I0073680

Bosses

Bosses

True Stories of
the Good, the Bad and the Ugly

Featuring first-hand reports, analysis,
and the eye-opening *Rate Your Boss* questionnaire

Roger D'Aprix

ChangeStart
PRESS

Library of Congress Cataloging-in-Publication Data

Names: D'Aprix, Roger M., author.
Title: Bosses: True Stories of the Good, the Bad and the Ugly / Roger D'Aprix.
Description: Seattle: ChangeStart Press, 2020.
Identifiers: LCCN 2019051893 (print) | LCCN 2019051894 (ebook) |
ISBN 9780983558873 (trade paperback) | ISBN 9780983558880 (Kindle edition)
Subjects: LCSH: Personnel management. | Leadership. | Work environment.
Classification: LCC HF5549 .D287 2020 (print) | LCC HF5549 (ebook) | DDC
658.4/092–dc23
LC record available at https://lccn.loc.gov/2019051893
LC ebook record available at https://lccn.loc.gov/2019051894

Published by ChangeStart Press
For information contact info@changestart.com

Author photograph by Richard D'Aprix
Printed in the USA by CreateSpace
Available from Amazon.com and other retailers

Copyright © 2020 by Roger D'Aprix
All rights reserved

For the panel of contributors,
who generously shared their good, bad and ugly boss stories.
You provide the credibility.

And for those bosses who willingly pay the price
of compassionate and caring leadership.

And, last but never least, for Theresa,
my most loving and generous boss.

ADVANCE PRAISE FOR *BOSSES*

Roger D'Aprix has once again helped us recognize the enormous impact of workplace communications and culture on our lives. He doesn't mince words in talking about "bosses" and profiling examples of exemplary and atrocious behavior within many organizations across the globe, highlighting the true financial and psychological costs of poor leadership."
—*Diane M. Gayeski, Ph.D., Dean, Park School of Communications, Ithaca College*

Bosses need to first rate themselves using D'Aprix's Boss-Rating questionnaire and then read this book. And business schools need to establish 'schools for bosses' using his simple, sensible and sensitive models. He reminds us that engagement is an employee choice; his book demonstrates how bosses can create work environments that earn engagement.
—*Jim Lukaszewski, Chairman, The Lukaszewski Group*

For any first time manager to senior executive, *Bosses* is rich with research and advice on how to unlock discretionary effort and boost productivity, morale and morality through authentic leadership. Powerful stories illustrate the good, the bad and the ugly in corporate America with the hope and intention by a gifted writer to inspire more of the good!
—*Colleen J Rooney, SVP & Chief Communications Officer, Signet Jewelers*

Individual bosses make or break the people who work for them. And collectively, they create the culture of the organizations they work for. No one knows more about corporate culture—and few know more about people—than Roger D'Aprix.
—*David Murray, Editor & Publisher, Vital Speeches of the Day*

D'Aprix reflects decades of experience in ways that every reader can apply to his or her own situation. This book is well worth a careful read.
—*Robert L. Dilenschneider, Founder & Chairman, The Dilenschneider Group*

In *Bosses*, Roger D'Aprix shines a light on the most critical factor in employee engagement and business success—how managers show up, or not, for their employees. Packed with real-life stories, *Bosses* clearly articulates the benefits and harms managers and leaders can generate in

an organization. He paints a clear and compelling picture of how a great boss shows up, and the undisputed difference it makes in the lives of employees and thus the organization itself.
—*Barbara Fagan-Smith, CEO, ROI Communication*

Using solid data and diverse contributory testimony, Roger D'Aprix takes a hard look at boss behavior and how it impacts people and business results. This book is an invitation to bosses to take stock of the urgency to put people first in a dramatically changing world.
—*Lise Michaud, Founder, IC Kollectif*

Roger D'Aprix has just published another book, *Bosses*, that should serve as required reading for every project, team and corporate leader.
—*Jim Shaffer, Author of* The Leadership Solution

Bosses face high expectations. Companies today expect them to have the inspirational fire of Churchill, the business acumen of Amazon founder Jeff Bezos and the empathy of Mother Teresa. D'Aprix gives them the space to be human while holding them strictly accountable to do better.
—*Mike Klein, ChangingtheTerms.com*

CONTENTS

Preface	11
About the Contributors	15
Roots of the Problem	17
Learning to Lead	17
The Need for Change	18
A Caring Boss	20
Entitled Authority	22
The True Believers	23
Roger the Exemplar	27
The Deficits	28
Witnesses for the Prosecution	31
Bad Boss Behavior	31
Lessons Learned	44
The Case for Change	47
Out With the Old and In With the New	47
Making the Case for Change	49
The Burning Platform	50
Changing Dysfunctional Behavior	56
Fit to Serve	59
Why Things Go Wrong	68
Dysfunctional Cultures	70
Hiding in the Weeds	72
Top Dogs	75
Fundamental Employee Information Needs	77
Good Dog	79
The Sum of Its Parts	86
The Remedy	89
Talent and Technology	90
Needed: A Radical Shift	90
Questions for Today's Boss	96
The Communication Leadership Model	98
In Conclusion	99
Appendix: The Rate Your Boss Questionnaire	101
Tabulation Key	103
Team Feedback	105
Taking Action	106
Making it Happen	108
Acknowledgments	109

PREFACE

Why a book on bosses? The short answer is that practically all of us have one. And they exert an inevitable and significant influence in our lives.

But the truly compelling reason is that radical workplace change is urgently demanding that bosses up their game. In the Digital Age, organizations require greater innovation and creativity than ever before in pursuit of their ambitious goals. Innovation is an organization's true competitive edge, and it relies heavily on the boss/employee relationship.

Moreover, today's bosses are managing a workforce that's better educated and more sophisticated than previous ones and, to put it bluntly, less likely to suffer fools gladly. Yet bosses have been historically short-changed when it comes to training, development, and ongoing support. This is an unforgivable neglect bordering on senior-leader malpractice.

This book is a study of this most important work relationship. It is an attempt to shine a light on boss behavior—the good, the bad, and the ugly. In many respects it's more fun to dwell on the latter two categories simply for comic relief. But the more serious purpose is to look for lessons in the inhumanity with which we sometimes treat each other.

But we also need to pay close attention to the good bosses, who serve as role models for the rest of us. That's a crucial role, especially when we are young, impressionable, and malleable.

You may wonder in passing about the use of the loaded word "boss" in the title and throughout this book. The answer is that regardless of the allegedly more participative world we live in as implied by neutral titles like manager, team leader, supervisor, or even facilitator, the truth is that employee talk is inevitably about "the boss." Also, whatever the formal title, the holders of power generally think of themselves as "the boss." So let's not kid ourselves about the relationship. Boss it is.

No doubt the boss plays a prominent role in our lives. We tend to tell stories about them. We lament their shortcomings to our spouses, family members, and friends. And at the same time, we work hard to gain their approval and recognition. In truth, despite their importance, little has been written about bosses or their impact on our work and even our personal lives. And yet they're the closest leaders to us.

Unless robots replace them, an unlikely event given the complex nature of human leadership, they will be with us for the foreseeable future. So we must determine the essential qualities of the good boss as the nature of our work continues to change profoundly.

Not to suggest that the role that bosses occupy is an easy one. They are often caught between conflicting pressures that leave them confused and frustrated. And there are always a certain number of—shall we say—"difficult" employees.

At times bosses are ordered to take leadership actions for which they have been given no rational explanation, leaving them only with an unsatisfactory "because I'm the boss" or "nobody tells me anything." Those answers undermine the boss and persuade team members that he is simply a figurehead with no capacity to protect their interests.

Why and *how* should you read this book? The "why" is simple. We need to finally acknowledge the importance of the boss role, which has changed from checker and task supervisor to motivator, engager, and sometime visionary.

It's a new set of requirements we have yet to fully recognize and validate. Lousy bosses undermine your performance and your ability to do your best work. They demotivate and disengage the people they're supposed to lead. And they are the primary reason people quit their jobs.

Those reasons alone justify emphasizing the importance of the role.

How you should read *Bosses* is by paying attention to how dramatically the workplace is changing and what that means for leadership at all levels. And special attention is needed at the junction where boss and team members meet.

As you read on, picture your own boss with all the strengths and weaknesses that you are only too well aware of. Then ask yourself the all-important question: Given the opportunity, would I choose to work for this person again?

I suspect that your answer has much to do with the quality of your life both on and off the job.

About the Contributors

The late David Berlo, one of the pioneers in the early days of discussions about communication inside and outside corporations, non-profit agencies, and educational institutions argued that leadership and communication were equivalents, that one could not take place without the other.

The people who comprise the panel of contributors are experts on the subject of leadership communication. They have lived Berlo's dictum in their work. Eleven of them, including the author, have achieved IABC Fellow designations, the highest honor bestowed on any of its eight thousand members by the International Association of Business Communicators. The other five contributors are all highly respected practitioners in the field and have deep experience in all phases of communication leadership from corporate strategy to speech writing to leadership development and coaching.

Collectively, they are the experts whose stories make this book come to life. And, not incidentally, their experiences represent the so-called "state-of-the-art" in the relationships of bosses and workers. For every story they offer—good, bad, or ugly—there are employees throughout the workforce with countless more that go untold, lost for fear of retaliation or the belief that no one cares.

ROOTS OF THE PROBLEM

Learning to Lead

The sad truth is that most of us learn to be bosses simply by observing other bosses in action. It's a rare organization that makes a deliberate effort to train and develop boss candidates. And it's even rarer for organizations to methodically define the characteristics of the ideal boss and then meticulously assess the fitness of a given candidate against those characteristics.

The Gallup organization, which more than any other group has studied the impact of bosses on employee behavior and engagement, claims that companies select the wrong candidate for boss positions 82 percent of the time. That's eight times out of ten. So if you have a bad boss, now you know that you're not an exception. Small consolation, but at least you know.

However, being a boss is also no bed of roses. Bosses are under constant pressure for results, are often saddled with conflicting priorities, and are regularly buried under a raft of administrative duties. As Mark Twain once observed about being tarred, feathered, and ridden out of town on a rail, "If it weren't for the honor and glory of the thing, I'd just as soon walk."

The same is true of being a boss unless you're naturally attracted to the idea of trying to get work done through others.

Or God forbid, perhaps you just like to boss others around. Which raises another question. Is the position of boss something created out of our evolutionary journey? Did the demands of tribal survival require leaders who could mobilize others quickly without argument? Probably yes. Does the "fight or flight syndrome" help explain the visceral reaction we have to bosses in our lives? That's also likely. If the existence of bosses is something preordained by evolution, transforming boss behavior may be much more of a challenge than some of us have believed.

Still, the changing nature of work clearly requires behavioral change on the part of both bosses and employees. Evolution aside, today more than ever we need enlightened bosses with human relations skills, such as listening and clear communication, to help us understand what changes mean for our lives and our futures.

The Need for Change

Today our various organizations desperately need talented people with ideas, people who can create innovative solutions to our problems, people who can inspire others to do the same. Those organizations also need bosses who have the courage to permit talented people to take risks without the paralyzing fear of failure and dire consequences.

Gallup estimates the collective cost of "lousy bosses" (their characterization) at $500 billion annually. Imagine the folly of ignoring a business problem of that scale. Aside from the financial cost, imagine also the lost opportunity costs of mismanaging the human talent: the primary asset of today's organizations.

On a daily basis, disengaged and indifferent workers alienate customers, hamper productivity, and withhold discretionary effort—all to their own detriment and that of their employers.

Almost everyone has a boss. They can be real and up close. These days they also can be virtual and as close as your cell phone or email. Or they can be a customer, a client, or a patient with demands you must satisfy.

One of my team members in my time as a corporate manager used to claim that "the boss makes the weather." I wasn't quite sure what he meant until I began obsessively observing their influence on the people they were bossing. It was then that I started slotting them simplistically, but factually, as Good, Bad, or truly Ugly.

Those three categories cry out for definitions, although in the end, the verdict is most likely in the eye of the beholder. Years of posing the question to employees of what makes a good boss have persuaded me that the first quality is trust. If you can't trust your boss, the relationship will go nowhere. Closely tied to trust is consistency. Words and actions must match. What you do must be consistent with what you say.

Listening is another biggie. People want to be heard and respected by people they respect in return. A Jesuit priest I knew once said to me that the two most beautiful love words in the English language were "uh huh." But the sad truth is that listening is our most poorly developed communication skill.

Still another quality of the Good Boss is simple kindness. Pfizer in its leadership development of company bosses puts it about as well as it can be said. One of the simple messages it sends to its bosses is: "Don't be a jerk." How poetic in its simplicity.

Finally, people say they want a coach—someone who can help them see their strengths and weaknesses and offer constructive advice. And they want someone who has the backbone to support them against the vagaries of corporate life when they deserve that support.

Bad Bosses, in my view, generally fall into one of two categories. Either they shouldn't have been selected in the first place or they are ignorant of what is expected of them in today's organizational world. In both of those cases, I blame their leaders for not paying attention to fundamental leadership-development issues. More to come on that particular neglect.

Bad Bosses are usually defined in terms of incompetence. He or she doesn't understand the work. They have no idea of what it is to lead. They play favorites. They let people to get away with actions that hurt the team. They refuse to stand up for us. They take personal credit for our accomplishments. And so on.

The Ugly Bosses are horses of a much different color. They are frequently just drunk with power, or they are natural-born psychopaths.

Ugly Bosses are the malevolent ones. They abuse their power. They throw tantrums when things go wrong. They punish us for *their* shortcomings. And they act irrationally and inconsistently, constantly keeping us in fear of losing our jobs. Think they don't truly intend to treat people badly? Think again. We'll look at a few cases along the way.

The rest is characteristic of any good relationship. No one wants to be another's patsy, subject to spoken and unspoken assaults on one's dignity. So the answer to being a good boss comes down to establishing and maintaining a healthy, positive two-way relationship with team members.

A Caring Boss

To set off on a deliberately positive note, I'm going to tell you about one of the really good bosses with whom I had the pleasure of working in the late 1970s into the early '80s. The '70s in particular were the halcyon days when Xerox was the darling of Wall Street.

His name was David Kearns, and he was the Xerox CEO in a period of intense company change as Xerox was getting its first taste of real competition. Two prime characteristics made him a good boss: his fairness and his concern for the people he led.

Like most senior leaders, he often found himself in conflicting positions. It was his job to obsess about shareholders, revenue and profit, and competition; but he had to do so in a way that respected company values and the people for whom he was responsible.

The best example I can offer of David's concern for people was Joe, my first Xerox boss. Joe was the kind of manager you either love or hate. From his days as a United Press reporter, he affected the brusque manner of the "reporters" in the famed Broadway play, *Front Page.*

One of his favorite stories from his younger reporting days was about a foot race to the nearest pay phone, long before the invention of cell phones, to call in a report to his editor of a news event he was covering. Racing to the pay phone, he tripped the middle-aged woman reporter running next to him. Down she went in a heap as his change clinked into the phone's coin slot. He always told that story with apparent glee.

Joe was also noted in the company for sending what were called "nasty-grams," barbed notes to peers and subordinates.

But it was mostly show. There was a certain softness to him that he usually kept well in check. You had to look to find it, but it was absolutely there.

In any case, Joe was struck with a slow-moving case of multiple sclerosis when he was in his 40s. He took the diagnosis remarkably well considering the inevitability of the disease. His main concern was how he was going to take care of his family and his young children as the disease slowly progressed.

He needn't have worried.

David Kearns made sure that whatever else happened in the company, Joe would always be employed at Xerox. But it was no charity case. At Joe's funeral in 2002, he was eulogized as the hard-working professional he had always shown himself to be. In an article that Joe entitled "Making Things Whole" in the September 27, 1992 edition of the *New York Times Magazine* about the challenges of his life, he included the following:

"Medically, I am now classified as a functional quadriplegic. I can't walk. I can't shake hands. I can't pick up a pencil. Signing my name is out of the question. It's impossible to feed myself. Brushing my teeth is a job for someone else. I can't get out of bed by myself. I can't shower by myself. I can't go to the bathroom by myself. I can't dress myself. If I slide forward in my wheelchair, I don't have the strength to straighten myself out. I can't read unless someone turns the pages. I don't drive. I don't visit people. I don't go to the theater." He ended with characteristic defiance: "But I can still work."

Despite all of his limitations, with the physical assistance of a special-needs male secretary, Joe was able to compensate for these devastating disabilities. And did more than just compensate: he did all of the research, interviewing, writing, editing, and production of a company magazine that went to every Xerox employee in the US.

None of that would have been possible without the support of a boss who valued both compassion and professionalism, not to mention courage. In short, a Good Boss who cared. But how is it that we see less and less of this kind of support in today's workplace? It's a perplexing question worth exploring, with deep and complicated roots.

Entitled Authority

To provide an answer, let's begin with one overwhelming reality perhaps best illustrated by the old joke about the Irish immigrant cop who explained to the citizen he had just conked on the head with his billy club, "It ain't because I hates you that I beats you. It's 'cause I have da aut'ority to do so."

This little bit of stereotype, politically incorrect as it is, exemplifies one of the causes of abuse by bosses who thrive on their perceived power.

The interesting question is where does this exaggerated sense of authority and entitlement over the destiny of others come from? In short, who or what made them the boss?

To provide an answer we have to go all the way back to the era of royal power and the popularizing of the Divine Right of Kings. That doctrine essentially proclaimed that a monarch is subject to no earthly authority, deriving his legitimacy directly from the will of God.

Accordingly, the king is not subject to the will of his people, the aristocracy, or any other group. The implication is that only God can judge an unjust king and that any attempt to dethrone him or restrict his powers is contrary to God's will and may even be sacrilegious.

That notion had its roots in the Catholic Church when the early popes, who were some of the first claimants, argued that their authority came directly from God. They claimed that they had conversed with the Holy Spirit and that Spirit had given them instruction to do such and such and that their authority was not to be questioned by mere mortals.

Of course, Abraham and Moses predated all of their claims. They evidently thought that God's affirmation was a handy leadership credential. The kings of the day also saw that approach as a pretty effective way to keep their subjects in line so they too claimed their authority was God-given.

It was only a matter of time before other institutions, including work organizations, would invent their version of Divine Right to suit their needs. Because it naturally led to the notion of a hierarchy of power beginning with God, the king, and others of authority, it evolved over the centuries into a cultural norm not to be questioned.

The boss was born!

But there was another side of the coin. It would require a docile public that had to be controlled through custom and laws. Authority, loyalty, and discipline were enshrined as crucial institutional values. A broad effort ensued over several centuries to institutionalize these three values in both our assumptions and our beliefs. The result would be the creation of the institutional parent and the institutional child, namely the boss and the rest of us. This, of course, is a vast oversimplification of the evolution of leadership authority, but it captures the result.

The final step was to create a sustaining structure. Again, the church was the model with its hierarchy of pope, cardinals, bishops, and parishes led by pastors. The pastor would become the leader closest to the people. Ordained and educated, he became a local figure with unquestioning authority.

All of that was supported by the notion of a chain of command to ensure discipline and order, and to maintain the status quo. Take a look at the organization chart of any corporation and you will see the same institutional structure replicated. All that remained was the need for a persuasive theory to rationalize the authority structure.

The True Believers

Now fast-forward to modern times. In a book first published in 1960 (McGraw-Hill) and entitled *The Human Side of Enterprise,* social psychologist David McGregor described two conflicting theories of worker motivation that he designated as "Theory X and Theory Y." He labeled Theory X as "authoritarian" and Theory Y as "participative." The two were polar opposites.

Theory X is essentially a workplace version of Divine Right and the authority that goes with it. For the Theory X true believers, it was all so obvious. Workers dislike their work. They have little motivation or pride of accomplishment. They avoid responsibility like the plague and require constant supervision. They must be controlled, forced, and threatened to do their work. As one cynical executive put it to me in all seriousness, "People only perform with a gun to their heads." Needless to say, such assumptions and beliefs are extremely powerful influences on the behavior of any boss who shares them.

The assumption is that workers need constant reward or punishment to perform. Hence, the carrot and stick approach to leadership. Hold out the possibility of rewards for conformity and productivity; inculcate fear and punishment for lack of performance. And tie it all together with the legal doctrine of employment at will, which basically gives the employer the right to fire people with or without cause. So the threat of arbitrary loss of one's job is always folded into the recipe.

Another noted psychologist, Harry Levinson, commented caustically in 1973 in his book *The Great Jackass Fallacy*, What do you put between a carrot and a stick? His predictable answer: a jackass.

A true believer in Theory X can do a mountain of damage if left to his or her devices. Unfortunately, most bosses have little or no accountability to senior leaders because of the layers of management between them. Middle management in general is disinclined to "interfere" with bad boss practices or behavior so long as things seem to be running smoothly, and so bosses are often left to their particular interpretations of their roles.

And those working under those bosses have usually learned that it's a mistake to challenge them for fear of both subtle and not so subtle retribution. The result is that workers must roll the dice with a new or a current boss (good, bad, or ugly) as a leader of company talent. The talent has to adapt to the style and behavior of the boss rather than the boss needing to conform to company policies and values in leading the team. It's a set-up for uneven or poor leadership practices.

Here's an egregious example. Ralph (not his real name) was a General Motors plant manager. His immediate subordinates once described him to me in a focus group.in which they cited a number of distressing episodes.

Episode one: One of Ralph's line workers, they reported, discovered that Ralph was fond of barbecued ribs. He decided to try to win Ralph's approval by sharing a favorite rib recipe. He waited for the opportune moment when Ralph was walking the factory floor and ensuring that production was going smoothly. Theory X managers are typically of the micromanaging mindset, and on this day Ralph had stopped to chastise an operator for taking a shortcut in a work process.

Seeing his opportunity to curry favor, the worker sidled up to Ralph with his recipe in hand. The two men chatted amiably, and Ralph expressed his appreciation for the new way to prepare his favorite meal. The next day he filed the paper work to fire the worker on the grounds that he had no business leaving his machine for a non-break social encounter.

Episode two: On another occasion on a Saturday morning's scheduled overtime, Ralph noticed that a secretary in his plant had parked her Cadillac in the row reserved for plant management. He was irked that she had taken such a liberty despite the fact that the row was empty with plant leaders mostly off for the weekend. He confronted her not only about the lapse in protocol, but he questioned her as to how she possibly could afford such a luxury car on her salary. She was gone within a week.

Episode three: There was also the time that Ralph heard rumors that his workers had hidden coffee pots in secret spots in the factory. He labeled them as "contraband" and announced that he would fire anyone who was found hiding one. He asked "spies" to turn in any co-workers who possessed forbidden items in and around their workstations. He promised anonymity.

Since no one took him up on his offer, Ralph, along with one of the company's security people, proceeded to break into all of the plant lockers looking for what he considered contraband. All sorts of personal items were confiscated, and the offenders were disciplined.

Are such antics typical in the workplace? Common maybe in some twisted corporate cultures, but there isn't any objective way to determine how common. These incidents are either covered up or simply tolerated by cowed employees afraid of retribution if they speak up. Still, there is enough anecdotal evidence of such boss behavior to suggest that it is more than an isolated phenomenon. This is the behavior I would certainly label Ugly. You will see some further examples as you read on.

It's time for an antidote to Ralph's Theory X behavior. McGregor wrote that Theory Y was a whole different kettle of fish. It posited that people are naturally proud of their work and their accomplishments. The trick is to provide a climate that nurtures their normal inclination to do good work without being micromanaged by a hovering boss. In the end, it's a matter of trusting people to do the right thing. The belief that reinforces that trust is that solving problems, overcoming challenges, and the work itself are intrinsically satisfying and motivating.

Both theories reveal their respective views of human nature. One sees people as essentially demotivated, directionless, and lazy. The other sees them as well intentioned, trustworthy, and inclined to identify with their work.

Ironically, Good Bosses can come from either school of thought. We've all seen the tough-minded autocrat who somehow earns the respect and undivided loyalty of the people he or she manages. I'm inclined to label them "X prime." Taciturn, slow to praise, but always pursuing the best interests of the whole, they inspire others with their fairness and dedication to results. It's the John Wayne model of the tough but benevolent leader.

And then there's the opposite: the permissive boss who is outrageously taken advantage of. Both stereotypes have led to a corporate bias that says, in effect, a boss has only two choices. Be tough and get results or be soft and get taken advantage of. It's a distorted dichotomy that leads to distorted behavior.

Jack Welch, the uncompromising CEO emeritus of General Electric, slotted his bosses in four quadrants according to how they lived GE's values. In reverse order, he identifies them as follows: Type 4, the tyrant who gets results while running roughshod over people and the company's values; Type 3, the boss who neither lives by the values nor gets results; Type 2, the benevolent boss who lives by the values but fails to get results; and his favorite Type 1, the boss who does both—lives the values at the same time they fully achieve their objectives.

Welch admitted that the tyrant who made the numbers (Type 4) was the hardest case because of the high value placed on results. But he noted that when GE began systematically removing such bosses, the company made "a great leap forward." The problem, Welch said, is that they have the power "to destroy the open, informal, trust-based culture we need to win." Our friend Ralph would never have made it under Welch's leadership.

Roger the Exemplar

Another memorable focus group subject was a mine boss named Roger. At a Zeigler Coal operation located in the coalfields of Illinois, his team was summoned from the coal mine to a company conference room to discuss the state of leadership at the mine. They ambled into the room in their coveralls and miners' helmets, which they put solemnly on the polished conference room table.

The mood was subdued with the unspoken question of "why the hell do we have to go through this silly exercise?"

After a few moments of trust-building and mumbled questioning of what this exercise was all about, they began to cautiously respond.

The open-ended question that really got their attention was, "How would you describe your team boss as a leader?" There was an audible shuffling of bodies as they looked from one to the other to determine how to respond. It wasn't so much that they didn't have an opinion but more like, "What is this all about? Why are they asking about Roger? Is he somehow in trouble?"

After a pause, one of the miners began to speak, almost defiantly. "Roger is the finest boss I've ever worked for. Whatever he tells you, you can take to the bank." Soon the others joined in, and the stories tumbled out one by one. "Like the time I got hurt and had to take time off. Roger covered for me and made sure no one would take a notion to fire me."

"Or the month we missed our quotas badly, and Roger went to management, explained why and took the blame personally."

Another added, "Roger never chews out one of us in front of the others. He'll take you quietly aside and ask what went wrong and how can he help solve any problems…"

"He's fanatic about safety," added another to a chorus of nodding heads. "He won't take any chances if there's the slightest possible risk to our safety…"

Summing it all up after 30 minutes or so of positive anecdotes, one miner added passionately, "I'd walk through fire for that guy!" Based on past experiences and the nature of the coal business, I had expected a very different experience from the one that was unfolding in this encounter. What was the difference from the grousing that so often characterizes employee focus groups?

Clearly, Roger was one of Jack Welch's Type 1 managers, a guy who lived company values at the same time that he achieved results. His numbers were consistently above those of his peers. The secret was that he had achieved what all of the HR experts long for, namely an engaged team willing to give of their discretionary effort, that reserve most of us keep to ourselves until or unless we're willing to unleash it for the greater good.

The Deficits

Ever since the arrival of global competition, work organizations have been enthralled with the possibility of unlocking that effort. If that were to happen on a massive scale, the possibilities for productivity and innovation would be practically limitless. But the catch is the need for impeccable leadership, especially at the boss level. In turn, that will require a far different mindset from the one possessed by the believers in Theory X.

Exactly what sort of transformation would be required to achieve that Nirvana? For one thing it would call for a massive training and development effort for which most organizations don't seem to have much appetite. As evidence, consider one of the few studies done on the extent to which major corporations treat the preparation and monitoring of bosses for their roles.

The sponsor of the study, ROI Communication, is a global consulting company headquartered in the Silicon Valley. More than 100 companies most likely to have the resources and the inclination to deal with the boss issue participated in that first benchmark study in 2013. The focus was how a boss typically perceives and carries on their communication role with their team. The premise was simply that effective communication is fundamental to effective leadership.

Here are the mixed, and somewhat alarming, findings.

- 49% of the companies surveyed rate their managers as effective in their communication leadership role;
- 70% of bosses don't understand the expectations of their leadership communication role;
- 23% of the companies define communication competencies for all people managers;
- 33% of leaders and managers get communication training;
- 24% are held accountable in their performance reviews for communication and leadership effectiveness;
- 58% of leaders and managers offer recognition for a job well done;
- 32% of leaders and managers explain company issues to their teams.

And those numbers come from some of the world's leading companies!

Given the above circumstances, it's not surprising that some 69 percent of bosses confess that they are "sometimes uncomfortable communicating with employees." A 2016 Harris Poll of over 2,000 U.S. adults that included over 600 bosses at various levels in their organizations showed that their leading discomfort was giving direct performance feedback. The fear had to do mainly with the possibility of "negative employee reactions."

The survey also revealed that many managers are afraid of being perceived as vulnerable (i.e., admitting mistakes), recognizing results, discussing company performance, giving clear directions, admitting that others have good ideas, and speaking face-to-face rather than using email.

In brief, taking on a true leadership role for which they are neither trained nor held accountable.

The late Stephen Covey, author of the 1989 best-selling *The 7 Habits of Highly Effective People,* studied employee understandings (presumably the other side of his boss findings). He found the following results tending to reflect the disturbing realities reported in the ROI Communication study:

- 37% of employees understand what their organization is trying to achieve;
- 20% are enthusiastic about their team and organizational goals;
- 20% have a clear line of sight from their contribution to company goals;
- 15% feel they are empowered to execute key goals;
- 20% trust their senior leadership.

The last finding is especially troubling: senior leaders are not generally trusted; immediate bosses get much better trust ratings. Familiarity does help to develop trust, but it seems clear that the behavior of senior leaders as a group doesn't. Their willingness to entrust company talent to ill-prepared bosses and to often decline to act on legitimate employee concerns may well be the reason.

In my own experience of conducting company-wide studies of leadership behavior, I have often felt that I was reading a suspense novel, a whodunit to expose the victims and the villains. Over time, it becomes strikingly clear who is who and why. And it holds up an undeniable mirror to senior leaders.

Let's take a peek.

WITNESSES FOR THE PROSECUTION

As part of the research for this book, I identified a group of leadership-communication experts to report what their experiences with various bosses have taught them about this most intimate and serious relationship.

All of those on the panel of contributors now work or have worked in sensitive positions with unique access to the leaders of the large companies they have counseled.

Bad Boss Behavior

For these first few stories I deliberately asked the panelists to report their experience with the darker side of boss behavior, because that's where the damage is done. Later we'll focus on a more diverse and positive view. The following stories in the panelists' own words have been edited only for length and clarity.

HOT FLASHES (OR WHO TURNED UP THE HEAT?)
By Jim Shaffer

The communication director for a Midwestern baking company, asked if I would help her conduct a performance improvement project at one of her company's bakeries.

The company had four bakeries in the upper Midwest. Our assignment was to assess which would best serve as a pilot to improve results by better managing communication among the various bakery units. We would then apply what we'd learned at the pilot plant to the other three plants.

Our assessment process consisted of individual interviews with members of the leadership teams followed by focus groups with salaried and hourly employees.

Three of the plants turned out to be relatively high-performing operations. We selected one based on the strength of the plant leader and his eagerness to lead a pilot effort. He was particularly interested in managing communication to improve business results.

The fourth plant was a recent acquisition, struggling to come back from a messy strike by a local union. Management and employees were at odds about new policies, procedures, and benefits. Both groups were forced to take pay cuts to get costs into line. All parties could best be described as surly as we conducted interviews and group discussions.

The first step in evaluating whether we could usefully apply lessons learned at the high-performing plant was to understand how its workforce felt about their jobs, and to explore their concerns, needs, issues, and ideas.

Before starting one of these sessions with hourly workers, Chuck, the plant manager, introduced Louise, my client, and me, then explained the meeting's purpose: "to listen to what's on your mind and ways we can improve."

Almost immediately things turned ugly.

"I can't believe you'd have the guts to ask us to tell you what's on our minds when we've been telling you what's on our minds since we were bought," an employee with a Green Bay Packers jersey shouted.

"Haven't you been paying any attention to us? Haven't you listened to a damn thing we've been telling you about?" a woman at one end of the table complained.

"You can start by getting the damned heat in this place turned off," a man shouted at Chuck. "Don't you know it's June and the heat in here and on the bakery floor is intolerable? No one should have to put up with this."

At that point Chuck got up from the table and said to the group, "I've heard all this before. We're doing the best we can. You people don't appreciate all that we're doing. I'm excusing myself. I'll meet with Louise and Jim and get a summary from them."

"Are you going to tell us what they say?" a soft-spoken young woman from the office staff asked Chuck.

"Yeah, yeah, I'll tell you," Chuck said unconvincingly.

And as he left the conference room, he mumbled under his breath, "They want to talk about heat, I'll show 'em some heat."

After a brief silence to let Chuck get out the door, we went back to facilitating our "so-called" focus group.

Mr. Green Bay Packers turned to Louise and me and said, "See what we mean? This place is horrible but there aren't many jobs in this town. Unfortunately, this is about it."

Another employee who had sat silent earlier said, "If they could just turn the air conditioner on. I bet we'd all be more civil."

Everyone nodded silently. And after an awkward pause, one of the employees looked anxiously at Louise and me and asked, "Do you think it's getting hotter in here than it was when Chuck was here or is it just me?"

"I feel it too," one of the employees offered. "I think the bastard went and turned on the heat again. That's what I think."

"It's definitely hotter," one said. And it was.

"Welcome to our world," said another.

We ended our meeting perhaps a bit prematurely, but no one was able to give us constructive feedback in the stifling heat of the room.

Back in Chuck's office, where the air temperature was blessedly cool, we sat down to offer a brief assessment.

"Did you enjoy the sauna?" he asked with a malicious grin. There was no doubt he had turned on the heat in an already volatile environment. Our interview was over.

My take: Aside from a deliberate bit of childish behavior from a miffed boss, what do we learn from this story?

The clearest lesson has to do with the boss's need to listen and respond appropriately so that words and actions match. People inevitably believe what they see and experience. They desire for leaders to care about their legitimate needs—in this case a tolerable work environment.

Their question: Does anyone care?

NEVER LOOK 'EM IN THE EYE, DAVE
By Stacy Wilson

Dave always had a television on in his office, presumably to stay abreast of news and markets. But it was often tuned to other types of content and was very distracting during meetings.

He also had the distressing habit of never making eye contact with women. All the women on his team talked about this behavior. It made us uncomfortable. It made me feel like a second-class citizen; someone he didn't take seriously. One day I popped into his office to ask a quick question. I noticed visuals on the television of people running away from a building. It looked like chaos. I asked him about it.

"Somebody is shooting up a school in Littleton, Colorado," he said dismissively, waving his hand toward the TV. He knew I was from Littleton. He knew I had family and friends in Colorado. As usual, he didn't make eye contact or deign to discuss the ongoing rampage. I turned and walked out of his office without asking the question that brought me there in the first place.

The event unfolding on that day was the Columbine High School shooting. I walked across to my own office, went in, closed the door, picked up the phone, and called the firm that had been trying to recruit me. I told them I was ready to take the offer. My current job no longer inspired me because of my diffident boss.

My take: This story tells us to know your employees, show them compassion when appropriate, listen to them, and give them your full attention—including eye contact—when interacting. In Western society, lack of eye contact is usually perceived as disinterest or dismissal, neither of which makes for cordial relationships or trust. Again, does anyone care?

MISTAKEN IDENTITY
By Anonymous

Ed was known to be the bully of the HR department. He loved nothing more than a good fight with his peers over some small issue that he would (as he often said) "take you to the mat" over. His team learned not to challenge him over anything, fearing an onslaught of anger and personal abuse.

No one dared to confront him. In fact, two or three indulged in a kind of Stockholm syndrome in which the captives learn to bond with their captor.

Ed ultimately imploded from his pent-up anger and died at a relatively early age. It was a shock that no one quite knew how to respond to—relief, sadness that his life ended in his prime, a feigned mourning? It was a confusing array of emotions.

The funeral was an elaborate gathering, with Ed's former rivals chosen to be pallbearers. There was even a eulogy or two praising his "wonderful qualities" and his achievements as a driven corporate executive. I was sitting in a pew with Brian, one of my fellow managers. Both of us harbored some animosity for Ed based on our past dealings with him as our boss. So our emotions, while listening to the effusive praise, were a mix of disbelief and anger at the hypocrisy.

Finally, I felt Brian's elbow jabbing me in the ribs, and I heard in a stage whisper the fateful words I've never forgotten.

"Good God. They're burying the wrong guy."

My take: In the workplace, as in life, you reap what you sow. This sort of leadership abuse is destructive of any semblance of the team spirit essential to team morale and productivity. With his inability to control his temper, Ed violated both the dignity and the engagement of his team, and perhaps even had an impact on his own mortality.

THE SHAME GAME
By Anonymous

The Vice President of HR reported to her team on a request from the Chief Operating Officer (COO) to find ways to strengthen teamwork and cross-division communication in this historically siloed organization. Several of those present commented on the irony that the COO was looking for culture change but had passed the task to HR. Individual initiative and results, and compet-itive behavior, were very much ingrained in the culture. This would clearly be a major challenge.

"We're to meet with him tomorrow to sketch out some ideas and a preliminary plan for moving forward. So I'd like you all to be back here at 5:00 p.m. and we'll work as late as we need to get something prepared. Okay with everyone?"

One individual spoke up: "I'm afraid I have a hard stop at 6:15 p.m.—picking up my daughter for her soccer game—but, of course, I'm good until then."

The group reconvened at 5:00 p.m. and began work—sometimes as a large group and sometimes breaking into smaller groups for a few minutes of brainstorming and idea sharing. Just before 6:15 p.m. the individual with the time constraint said, "I'm at my stop time, but I'll be online tonight and add more to what's developing; and I'll be in extra early tomorrow to pick it up again."

The VP looked at him with evident impatience and dismissal. "All right, I guess."

The passive aggressive behavior and tentative permission and annoyance in her response was evident to all. She added with un-disguised sarcasm, "Enjoy your evening off." The implied follow-on message of "while the rest of us have to stay here and work" went unspoken.

My take: This is a crystal clear demonstration of how the leader can set the tone. Her sarcastic shaming sent a clear message to all in the room that family-friendliness wasn't part of the culture.

Contributor Dave Johnston tells a similar story of "being guilted" except that his experience was perhaps worse. He was slated to introduce the main speaker at a company-sponsored meeting and give a brief presentation to the leaders of the Houston business community when he was faced with a painful conflict. His newly adopted baby daughter was arriving from South Korea on the same day as the meeting.

He did what he believed was the logical thing and informed his boss that he would happily prepare a peer to fill in for him. The boss, who happened to be head of the company's Work and

Family task force, demurred warning Dave that this was "an important career opportunity."

"Do you have to go? What would be so wrong about your wife going to the Los Angeles Airport and picking up the baby instead of you?"

Dave's response was "I think my daughter's arrival is more important." The appointed head of work/family balance replied, "I think you ought to really reconsider." To his credit Dave made the trip to Los Angeles to welcome his new daughter.

Guilt is the primary tool of manipulation. In both of these cases, it was more than a missed opportunity to support a clearly communicated parental priority. In the first case it was a deliberate shaming in front of his co-workers, a tactic that diminishes the recipient while it discomforts and embarrasses those who witness it. In the second case it was a matter of an inflexible boss offering the lesson that work/family balance takes a back seat to other priorities.

Either way it is a negative reply to "Does anyone care about my parental obligations?"

BAD TIMES IN THE LAND OF COTTON (NOT FORGOTTEN)
By Stacy Wilson

During my last week on the job at a former employer, the then-CEO decided to roll out a change to the employee dress code: cotton pants were now banned. I was asked to craft the communication messages to employees announcing the revised policy.

But I was not allowed direct access to the CEO. Had I been able to counsel him, I'd have asked these questions:

- How do you intend to police the no-cotton-pants code?
- Is a blend (e.g., cotton/polyester) ok?
- Would we supplement employees' clothing budgets to purchase more expensive clothing in linen, wool, rayon, or silk?
- Would we be covering employees' dry cleaning bills for items they cannot wash at home?

- Do our uniforms in the field, food service, and the stores comply?

I imagined the clothing police stopping employees in the hallways: "Show me your tag."

I cautioned my boss and his boss that this would be poorly received and likely to go public. They ignored my pleas to counsel the CEO to reconsider. The announcement went out. The next day, it showed up on the front page, as the day's lead story in the nationally known and well-respected local paper.

My take: CEOs who thrive on arbitrary and poorly considered actions usually pay a price. Like the infamous Captain Queeg in *The Caine Mutiny*, they subject themselves to ridicule and anger which ultimately causes resistance to their own authority. Worse is the conclusion that such leaders will happily exercise that authority even when it defies common sense.

THE PRAISE TRAP
By Anonymous

As a director of the firm, I had been instrumental in recruiting and hiring a young team leader who very quickly established herself as a real asset, a leader with great energy and talent.

She put tremendous effort and many late hours into pursuing and eventually winning a major client. In the process she engaged people from other regions, who could bring the right mix of skills and experience.

It was a true team effort.

Her boss—the regional manager—had a reputation for preferring the power of the stick rather than the carrot of incentives. So when I sent an email congratulating the team and its informal leader I wasn't exactly surprised at the boss's response when I ran into him a few days later at a company meeting.

He called me aside and offered a disappointing reaction to the email. In his words, "Too much of this 'great job' stuff just encourages them to ease up."

The managers who operate from this sad premise are everywhere. The notion is that if you provide praise or recognition of any kind, you risk "spoiling" the employee's motivation to do good work and impress you. It's the keep 'em guessing school of leadership, and it's dead wrong. Recognition for true performance is itself a motivator.

My take: Lord knows where this belief comes from—that withholding recognition makes people try harder. My guess is that it's a product of a negative childhood experience with a low-reacting or over demanding parent. Whatever the cause, it is contrary to people's need for performance feedback and especially for recognition.

PARDON OUR APPEARANCE
By Roger D'Aprix

One look said it all. The setting was a focus group at a leading aerospace company in the East. The assembly-line employee walked into the conference room, settled heavily into a chair at the end of the table, and sighed loudly to signal that he was there under protest.

He was a large man sporting a baseball cap he never removed. As the room filled with other participants, he closed his eyes and slumped further down into his chair. For the next 75 minutes, he remained completely silent.

I had a series of questions to pose to the group about the effectiveness of supervisory leadership at the sprawling facility. There had been quality issues on the production line, and the senior leadership wanted to know how seriously the issue was being addressed by supervision.

As part of the quality campaign, company bosses were instructed to carry on discussions with their people about the criticality of the problem.

To highlight the communication, company leadership had hung huge banners on every building. They offered words to the effect of "Quality is our most important priority." Leaders often believe in simple solutions to complex problems. So they wanted to know how employees were reacting to the banners.

I posed the question to the group. Silence.

Finally, the man in the baseball cap was aroused. He looked at me with disdain, pushed at the peak of his cap to better make eye contact, and announced with scorn, "Buddy, you can believe two signs around here regardless of what the bosses are saying.

"One says 'Wet Paint' and the other says 'Pardon our Appearance.' All the rest is bullshit."

My take: I've always appreciated blue-collar employees for their inclination not to mince words when asked provocative questions. This was no exception. There's an inviolable social research principle that says "if you don't want to hear the answer, don't ask the question." Too often senior leaders rely on simplistic tactics (think posters and banners) to resolve complex issues. It's no surprise that such "answers" have little or no impact and instead serve only to increase employee skepticism about leadership naiveté.

DUNG & DONE
By Pixie Emslie

I had been a senior newspaper reporter in South Africa and the UK through the 1970s but in 1981 decided to leave the newsroom to venture into corporate communication. It was a good move and I had some wonderful times working as a motoring journalist for a small independent company, and later editing in-house publications for one of South Africa's big mining companies.

Eventually, I took up the position of Head of Internal Communication at Eskom, South Africa's power utility, with about 50,000 employees.

I had a staff of 20 people, including translators (we worked in four main official languages), the photographic and video departments, writers, admin, and editors at Head Office, and I was in charge of communication at 10 power stations, as well as numerous substations and all the offices of what we termed Distribution, the people who tended the massive power line system that criss-crosses the country.

What a time we had. We produced an eight-page tabloid newspaper every fortnight, completely replicated in English and Afrikaans; we produced a fun-filled and informative Eskom Video News replicated in four languages, once a month; and we introduced competitions to encourage excellent customer service.

It was a wonderful few years, working with people who could influence the work lives of thousands of employees. We had heartwarming results and enthusiastic response. The thing that made it all worthwhile was knowing that we were making a difference. For example, I once discovered that men working on one of the pump storage stations had no idea that the work they were doing underground, where the great turbines were kept in perfect condition by them, was actually producing electricity!

My gratitude went to my superiors, who were excellent leaders, giving me in senior and middle management every encouragement and support to run with the projects we developed. Until there was a new manager appointed over our staff. Koos (not his real name) had not the slightest idea of what our work was about. He came into this vibrant department like a bull in a china shop, reorganizing all the assignments, changing departments around, even moving our translators into a different section of the building.

There was a lot of unhappiness. My senior editor resigned when Koos censored her story about an embarrassing breach of safety regulations. The head of the video department was told he had to feature the new manager in our monthly video news—but Koos was neither good on camera, nor good at presenting—and to make it worse his English was so strongly accented that he was hard to understand.

Dislike of the man was so intense that someone even put a big ball of elephant dung in a box on his desk that they had brought all the way from a game reserve. One day when I had one of many confrontations with him, he took me off to a room I had not even known existed—to "talk in private" so that we wouldn't be overheard. It was basically a windowless cell, and to my horror he locked the door behind him before starting to tell me how full of myself and how poor a leader I was. It shocked me to the core and I left the building in tears.

It didn't take me long to see one of the senior Directors and pour my tale of woe out to him. But things only went from bad to worse; now I was responsible for having Koos hauled over the coals by his superiors.

It could not go on and, encouraged by my husband, I resigned with my only plan being to "go it alone" and work from home. That was the start of a new 15-year career as an independent consultant that brought me into contact with new people, places, and experiences all over the world. So in the end, one really, really ugly boss forced me to quit and change direction. Sadly, that wasn't the case for everyone—the department disintegrated, and our former accomplishments were all undone.

My take: I have never understood why any ill-tempered boss believes they have the right to berate an employee either privately or publicly. Performance feedback requires the art of tact and diplomacy together with polite candor. Here we have an example of a failure on both counts: tactlessness and even the threatening gesture in locking the door. Was the boss actually hinting at physical harm?

Years of team accomplishment were undone by the behavior of a vain and vindictive boss.

TRASH-TALKIN' MAMA
By Anonymous

Early in my career I took a job at a small advertising and PR agency. It paid next to nothing, but I was promised the opportunity to work on the creative side in addition to a healthy set of administrative responsibilities.

My manager "Lisa" was a nice woman, but I soon learned that her manager, "Lana," made the decisions and controlled the environment we were all part of.

She often kept our 15-member team waiting before she joined her Monday morning standup meetings. We were forbidden to leave the room even though she could keep us waiting up to 45 minutes and sometimes never showed up at all.

All these years later and I still think of those meetings as some of the worst I've ever experienced. When she entered the room, everyone was silent, waiting for her to choose her victim. Every week someone was in the line of fire, and she would pepper them with questions and criticisms. Sometimes they left the room crying.

Some mornings she would swoop in and announce, "I'm in a bad mood so if there's anyone who can't deal with that, you can go home now."

After she fired a guy who actually went home, I understood that her proclamation was simply a way to notify us that it was going to be a terrible day. Everyone would put their heads down and try to appear invisible, but when she was on the rampage there was no way to hide.

As time went on, she often reviewed my press releases and ad copy, covering them with red ink until the page looked like evidence of a grisly accident. Then she'd summon me, fling the paper on the floor, and tell me to pick it up. While Lisa told me I was doing good work, Lana said "if the day ever came that I pulled my head out of my ass, she'd have to be resuscitated."

One morning I came in to find that the janitors hadn't taken out the trash the night before. Lana announced to the team that I would take out the trash because I wasn't qualified to do anything else. Much to my surprise, I refused. "I wonder how you'll feel doing cold calls," she asked as she slammed a stack of leads on my desk. "I expect some new business by tomorrow."

I quit the next day.

My take: Here is another outrageous story of abusive boss behavior. Again, one wonders where people in authority get the notion they have a right to humiliate another human being simply because that person is subject to their authority. Plain human decency, if not corporate custom, should dictate otherwise. How much talent is lost daily from such episodes? How many high-performing employees get their fill of such behavior and quit—either literally or passively—by simply vowing to withhold their energy and commitment?

Lessons Learned

So where do these stories leave us? Many Theory X bosses would say that they portray the whining of a few entitled employees who should be just glad they have a job. They ask why these people don't understand that it's a cold, cruel world out there and that nobody gives a damn about their personal struggles with authority. They'd tell them to get a grip, to grow up and see things as they are, not as they want them to be.

Those Theory X bosses would be offended that people have the nerve to complain or report abuse of authority. Indeed, the commonplace character of many of these stories paradoxically can easily invite a dismissive shrug.

But we're not living in the 19th or even 20th century with entrenched autocracy and hierarchy. Instead, we live in an intensely competitive global economy with human talent, innovation, and imagination as the primary source of competitive differentiation.

Today's successful companies often point to their ability to disrupt markets with unanticipated solutions and unforeseen products and services. Think Apple, Microsoft, Uber, Google, and Amazon. These companies and their leaders understand that the world has changed and that people are no longer merely a cost of doing business; that indeed they are the engine that determines success or failure. The once hollow boast that "people are our most important asset" has now become an all too obvious fact of business life.

Take a step back and look at these stories and the damage inflicted: examples of outright meanness showing "who's the boss around here," edicts and dress codes that have nothing to do with business effectiveness, and unnecessary loss of talent through bad boss behavior that persuades people to quit jobs they love.

The stories represent a reality that too often is hidden from view. The experiences reported here are replicated in different terms over and over again in the workplace. So the truly effective bosses—those who build authentic relationships and productive teams—appear to be the exception and not the rule.

It's hard to generalize about their numbers because their behavior—along with their 'opposites'—is hidden behind many a senior executive's disinclination to oversee boss behavior. So the typical boss is often left to rely on instinct and past experience with authority figures, making it up as they go along.

In the next chapter we'll look at the truly pressing issue—the urgent case for change.

THE CASE FOR CHANGE

The case for change can actually be stated in a few phrases: an ever-evolving corporate world; an increasingly diverse and aware workforce; the need for innovation and creative thinking in a global marketplace; a need for leaders who comprehend how the past must yield to the future. But that's the short version. The longer version is a bit more complicated.

Out With the Old and In With the New
Historically, it's fair to say that employee needs were given short shrift in the old industrial economy. Let's look at the contrast just in the changes in the nature of work and the workplace itself since then. The typical employee in the old manufacturing economy worked in a noisy factory ranging in cleanliness from untidy to downright dirty. It was often dominated by moving assembly lines with roving supervisors constantly checking the workflow to ensure speed, product quality, and uniformity.

In some heavy industries like steel manufacturing, automobile production, and mining, the work was often backbreaking and dangerous, posing both safety and health hazards. Long hours, sweatshops, child labor, and low wages were common. The culture was often one of mutual distrust and restrictive work practices. Management and labor relations were even marked with occasional outbreaks of violence between workers and private security forces. In short, work in the not too distant past was not the mostly antiseptic experience it is today.

In that industrial era, the worker was regarded merely as a cost of doing business. And the boss was a figure to be respected, catered to, and even feared. His power was close to absolute in leading what were referred to as "his people."

Happily, we've come a long way from those dark days. Today's work environment features an entirely different kind of manufacturing by a very different workforce. Largely, it's the use of information as the raw material to be transformed into useful knowledge for new products and services. The so-called knowledge worker, whether a software programmer, a call-center person, a trainer, a product designer, an engineer, or a boss, earns a living through their ability to apply their knowledge and experience to defined needs.

Today's workers, in general, are much less likely to be expending physical labor, nor are they merely a cost to the bottom line. As the saying goes, "today's company assets ride the elevators." This reality is no less true of blue-collar workers, who are being challenged to learn and use new technologies and work in more efficient and productive ways—or lose out to automation.

It is this transformation of work coupled with a more diverse and more sophisticated workforce that is largely responsible for requiring a new kind of boss. One who exhibits all of the requirements set out by Gallup and other researchers—people who have the human relations skills and talent to motivate, listen actively, and interpret complex business issues and decisions in terms that are meaningful to team members. And people who can handle the pressures and the contradictions of the job. Easy to say, not so easy to do.

The question presents itself as to whether these same requirements apply to blue-collar bosses. Or are they only for bosses who lead knowledge workers? The respective cultures that typify different types of work certainly influence boss behavior. But the hard reality is that we are really talking here about human needs at work regardless of the nature of the work itself Everyone deserves civility, respect, and the right to be valued as a human being.

Roger, the mine boss at Zeigler Coal, intuited that and acted on it to create one of the most positive work teams I've ever seen. He didn't have a Harvard MBA or anything like it. He was simply a decent soul who respected the miners, and who reciprocated by out-producing every other team in the company.

Revolutionary economic change that will only intensify is our lot in life. We have to understand and embrace it and learn to adapt to all of its demands if we are to have a healthy society in a global marketplace. The nature of the work has little or nothing to do with this reality.

Making the Case for Change

Yet there are always the counter pressures of inertia and denial. One of the folk sayings of the deniers and resisters is, "If it ain't broke, don't fix it." The argument is that people naturally dislike change; that they prefer to live with things as they are than undergo the risks and inconvenience of change.

The truth is that people will generally accept change if they perceive that it's driven by a compelling need and in the organization's best interests.

Yet some changes are obviously more difficult to accept than others. Large-scale change involving the need for an organization to confront and cope with a changing world is obviously considerably more challenging. In those instances, the case for change has to be made fully and persuasively starting at the top and cascading through the organization.

If the change somehow appears threatening or risky, there is likely to be resistance, even outright denial. The examples of that resistance and its consequences just from the recent past could fill a book of business lessons learned.

In my hometown—Rochester, New York—alone you can find two classic cases. Eastman Kodak is a poster child for such denial as is my old employer, Xerox. Into the early 1980s, Kodak employed more than 65,000 people in its sprawling Rochester, New York industrial park, the largest in the Northeast.

But like so many company towns, Rochester has seen those jobs evaporate as a disruptive digital imaging technology took over Kodak's formerly invulnerable market share. Today those 65,000 jobs are down to fewer than 5,000.

Likewise, Xerox once employed 15,000 people in Rochester. Today copier and printer manufacturing in Rochester employs half of that number. The 32-story downtown headquarters building, once a proud symbol of Xerox success and Rochester prosperity, has been totally vacated by the company. The final insult was the removal of the bright red Xerox logo from the façade and its unceremonious delivery to a local dump.

Disruptive technology, strong competition, and serious leadership miscues have reduced the company to a shadow of itself, ripe for the corporate raiders contemplating its future as an asset to be broken up and sold or as someone's takeover target at a bargain price.

Xerox stood idly by as others appropriated the technologies that they had pioneered. Exhibit number one: the personal computer that Apple and Steve Jobs ultimately developed and leveraged for its ride to glory. Instead, Xerox leaders saw its future as "the Document Company" and rode that wave to near disaster.

Kodak and Xerox made what turned out to be half-hearted attempts at transformation, but their leaders ultimately lost their nerve and their way. Hubris was the substitute for innovation. A dismayed senior leader expressed Kodak's ultimate excuse. He asserted that Kodak was "a chemical company dedicated to the film business, not a digital company."

The result of that denial was bankruptcy and the once unimaginable act of demolishing the buildings that housed Kodak's cash cow, its film production lines.

The Burning Platform

A popular metaphor for overcoming such change inertia and rationalizing large-scale corporate change is the "burning platform" story. Countless numbers of leaders have used the story to help persuade themselves and their stakeholders to accept significant change.

This metaphor for justifying radical change actually originated from the work of consultant and author Daryl Conner. A story in his 1992 classic, *Managing at the Speed of Change* went viral almost as soon as the book was published.

Conner was looking for a compelling way to express how leaders should look at crises, understand their options, and ultimately make the difficult decision to take on the risks of radical change. Four years before the book's publication he had seen a news account of the experience of one Andy Mochan, who was a supervisor of the crew on an oil rig in the North Sea off the coast of Scotland. On a tragic July evening in 1988, there was an explosion that killed 166 crewmembers on the rig, and two rescuers. Andy was one of 63 survivors.

As Andy later told the story, he remembered being awakened by the explosion and the alarms. Despite his injuries, he somehow managed to get to the edge of the platform from which he jumped 15 stories to water so cold that he could survive for 20 minutes at most if he weren't rescued.

When Andy was asked in the hospital why he decided to make that fatal leap, his answer was simple, "It was either jump or fry." He jumped because he felt he had no choice. He believed that the cost of staying on the platform was certain death.

In his analogy, Conner makes the point that leaders facing the need for major change often delay action until the existing conditions become unbearable. He emphasizes that for significant change to happen, leaders have to reach a point of "tenacity and unyielding commitment."

In other words, they must have the will over time to pursue the change regardless of how long or how painful the journey. Even good bosses may blanch at the prospect and lose their nerve. When they do, the outcome is usually a disaster for the organization and its employees.

At the lower levels of an organization, bosses obviously face a different set of challenges from those at more senior levels, although those challenges typically have their roots in senior leadership decisions and actions. The problem is that senior leaders too often neglect to share their logic and their perspective with the rest of the organization. It's easy for the senior leader to presume that everyone knows what they know and understands the case for change, a "fact" that is simply not true and that should never be presumed.

Most leaders are good at explaining the "what" of their decisions and actions, but they are pitifully bad at explaining the "why." Some of that is a penchant for secrecy and uneasiness about transparency. Some is a simple reluctance to share their motives for a given action. When decisions and actions are delivered without context, the boss is then left to interpret and explain to the team what a given decision means and why it is being made. Too often that leads to sheer speculation and misinformation.

Whenever such a vital decision or action is announced, people at the team level are interested primarily in answers to the following questions:

- Why is this being done?
- What does it mean for our team?
- How will it affect me now and in the future?

In an unpredictable, insecure workplace people want answers and context. That means turning all eyes outward to the marketplace and to the forces that rationalize company strategy. Making those connections is an imperative senior leadership task.

At the boss level, it means bringing the issues down to earth and interpreting what they mean for work teams in terms of their priorities and challenges. It also means, insofar as possible, explaining what those issues mean to and for the average company worker. Otherwise, how can those workers assess their future prospects, and how can they manage both their expectations and their careers?

In general, company leaders are getting better at information transparency, but there's still a very long way to go. If bosses are to be relied on to provide context for decisions, they need three things: first, the information to do the job; second, permission to be open with team members; and third, the understanding that this is a vital part of their responsibilities.

Here are two contrasting panelist stories in that regard. The first speaks to the benefits of "servant leaders" (i.e., bosses who defines their role as serving both the needs of the organization and the people they are leading). The second shows the folly of requiring good performers to adapt to poor leadership. It also demonstrates the need to be diligent in institutionalizing norms for leadership behavior and open communication rather than leaving such matters to personal leadership style or choice.

MY BEST BOSSES—TWO SERVANT LEADERS
By Angela Sinickas

Ron Musil and his boss, Pete Heraty, the VP of Employee Relations at the *Chicago Tribune*, were two of a kind. What made them amazing bosses is that they gave each of their staff a vision of what we were trying to accomplish in support of the *Tribune*'s strategic goals, expected us to figure out how to do our own parts in fulfilling it, and provided needed resources like external and internal training opportunities. They checked in with us once a month for progress reports and were always available if we needed advice or help in dealing with another department, but they never micro-managed.

Here's an example of how they supported their staff. The company announced it was building a new production facility and converting from hot-metal letterpress printing to computerized layout and offset printing. These days, we would call it a major change management challenge.

Since I was new to the company, I started asking employees what their questions or concerns about the new plant might be. I put this together in a chart, which showed that the issues were different for the hourly (mostly male) production workers moving to the new plant and the salaried (mostly female) office employees.

I was surprised that the office staff, who were staying in Tribune Tower, had concerns of their own. When I shared my findings with Ron, he and Pete recommended that I present the results to the task force planning the move.

I was in my early 20s, and was impressed and excited that they trusted a new, young staffer not to embarrass them, and that they didn't insist on making the presentation themselves. Based on some of the unanticipated findings of my research, changes were actually made to the blueprints of the new plant—and I was invited to become part of the task force.

Ron conducted meaningful performance reviews and provided immediate feedback, both positive and negative, throughout the year as projects were underway, long before Kenneth Blanchard and Spencer Johnson's *The One Minute Manager* was published (in 1986). They both were genuinely caring human beings whose impact and trust were felt well beyond professional accomplishments.

My take: The notion of the servant leader is exactly what our contributor states: "If you hire the right people and point them in the right direction, while providing a safety net of training and other resources, they and the entire department (will) succeed." It's a credo of faith in human nature led in the spirit of trust. In brief, a leader who serves rather than expects to be served and in the process elicits true engagement.

MR. X: ON A DESTRUCTIVE MISSION
By Angela Sinickas

My ugly boss story from another organization features a man who was hired as the new manager of HR with a charge to break the union. He had done this at his previous employer. The new boss, Mike, was a classic Theory X manager who believed that employees dislike work and do as little as possible to get by. He replaced a great Theory Y boss who had built a strong team of self-starters.

Mike set the stage at the first staff meeting of his tenure by telling us that after he graduated from college on a Friday, he got married on Saturday and started his first job on Monday. The lesson was not lost on us. Work was his priority. Then he laid out his ground rules:

- We were to take no initiative. We had to check with him before we made any decisions to take new actions beyond normal day-to-day transactions.
- We were not to expect him to keep us informed about high-level issues he was privy to, and weekly staff meetings would be reduced to once per month. He would tell us only what he thought we needed to know.
- He would handle anything that involved a conversation with vice presidents or the CEO; we were not to make any direct

contact ourselves. If one of the senior leaders directly called us, we were allowed to respond. However, we were to inform him immediately about the nature of each interaction.

- All training and professional development for our department was suspended.
- We were to remain at our desks every day until 6 p.m. whether or not we had work to do. He wanted anyone passing by to assume we were all working hard.

Managers and professionals in HR who had been working for years with a great deal of autonomy were shocked. As they watched Mike bully and undermine the formerly high-performing HR staff, they began to leave for other positions. I was among them.

After I left, the business experienced a prolonged and contentious strike resulting in a partial but divisive win for Mike's hostile and confrontational negotiating strategy. And following his own his departure, his successor (a Theory Y manager) had to rebuild the group. The destructive cycle was complete.

My take: These two contrasting stories illustrate the never-ending employee question: What's my job? In short, what are your expectations as my boss? What are the boundaries? Too often these questions are left unanswered and presumed. Or (as in the second story) an abusive boss distorts the answers.

In the first case those boundaries were broadly defined and were based on trust. In the second they were narrowly defined and reductive, sending a clear message of mistrust and suspicion.

The turnover rate says it all at considerable cost to the organization in loss of productivity and valuable experience. Not to mention the emotional upset of requiring people to adapt to an unfit and divisive boss who engineered a hostile work climate. But perhaps the greatest cost in such cases is to customer relations and service. Think about the fact that the only safe target for a discontented employee is the customer standing in front of them. Wonder why there is so much indifferent customer service these days? You need only observe how the company's employees are treated to understand.

Changing Dysfunctional Behavior

Here's a final nagging question senior leaders and bosses must confront. How intractable a problem are the bad bosses in today's workplace? How much of their behavior is a product of their personal demons and their need to dominate others? It's important to ponder the question of realistic transformations, or epiphanies, as we like to call them.

Gallup and other researchers make it clear that selection is the first rule of leadership. If only 10 percent of us have the necessary qualities for leadership, logic requires that we first identify and select that one in ten when choosing leadership candidates. But the same studies also emphasize that another two in ten can lead *if* they are properly trained and developed for the job.

Those facts dictate that HR professionals address the task of finding reliable ways to predict leadership success. In a time of sophisticated psychological testing and documented performance histories, that doesn't seem to be too much to expect.

Obviously, it's quicker and easier to rely on hunches, but a rereading of some of the horror stories reported here with their negative outcomes shows the folly of using hunches to predict successful boss candidates. As for the two in ten who might succeed with the proper training and development, that's ultimately a matter of senior leaders setting priorities and properly investing in talent development

Accountability based on fair evaluation and employee feedback is likely what makes the difference. Bosses who believe that they will be held responsible for abusing people in a fair management-accountability system will surely pay attention. That accountability should include removal from a leadership role and, if necessary, firing. The idea that employees must accommodate leadership behavior regardless of outcomes needs to be reversed.

If companies are serious about nurturing and retaining human talent, it's time to hold bosses accountable for excellent leadership as well as financial results.

An enlightened CEO once said to me, "We give them (bosses) a set of performance goals and a bag of money to manage, and if they screw up either one, we replace them. The same needs to be true of the talent we entrust to them. If they screw it up, likewise we should deal appropriately with them." As far as changing the behavior of bad leaders, he simply said, "Let's stop trying to do the impossible."

He added that when one of his direct reports comes to him with a request to stage a major downsizing, he responds with, "Okay, you're first. Who's next?" He continued, "Such requested actions represent a management failure. You'd be surprised how few such requests come across my desk."

Let's look next at what it takes to create and maintain an environment that supports real innovation and creativity as well as some opposing examples.

FIT TO SERVE

Based on more than three decades worth of researching the employee-engagement levels of 35 million employees globally, Gallup has consistently found that only one in three U.S. employees is fully engaged in their work.

On a global basis, it's worse with an engagement level of less than one in six. Gallup minces no words in blaming lousy bosses for the engagement deficit.

To remedy that deficit, they call for a new breed of boss—one who exhibits the following prescribed behaviors:

- They motivate every single employee to engage by providing a compelling vision and team mission.
- They have the assertiveness to drive outcomes and the ability to overcome adversity and resistance.
- They create a culture of clear accountability.
- They build relationships that create trust, open dialogue, and full transparency.
- They make decisions based on productivity, not politics.

The inevitable question is where will we find these paragons and what is it that makes the difference that marks their ability to perform according to this prescription? The pioneering researcher and leadership guru David Berlo always insisted that leadership is essentially about communication.

In fact, his belief was that leadership *is* communication and that effective leaders were typically effective communicators. Of course, leadership is more than good communication skills, but nearly all of the prescribed leadership behaviors above are impossible without those skills.

Besides exceptional communication skills, there is a triumvirate of other requirements. They come down to selection of the right candidates in the first place; well-designed leadership training; and ongoing mentoring and development. And let's not forget defining and enforcing measures of accountability consistent with the organization's reward system. To put it bluntly, that means recognizing and rewarding the good bosses and dealing appropriately with those who prove themselves unfit.

Here are real-life examples—both good and bad—illustrating the essential leadership triumvirate of selection, training, and development.

SINK OR SWIM
By Pixie Emslie

Belinda had a promising career as a journalist, with several years of experience at various newspapers and magazines in South Africa and the UK. She decided to try something new and joined an advertising agency as a senior writer. She couldn't say why except that it sounded glamorous, and it was a fast-moving world of creative people. Or so she thought. In reality they turned out to be hard drinkers, hard workers, and hard people.

So when a post was advertised at the University of the Witwatersrand in Johannesburg, she applied and was hired. She would be Head of the Department responsible for producing a weekly newspaper for all the academic and administrative staff in addition to press liaison, radio, TV, and other publicity.

At the age of 28 and full of confidence, she entered this new world of some 30,000 students and several thousand staff ranging from senior professors to the people who maintained the grounds and buildings. The department included a staff of 12.

The first problem she encountered on Day One was a secretary—an older woman who had a strong aversion to "having a boss who was still a child." She took early retirement and left. Of the rest, most were older than Belinda. Quite a few had been there for years, were set in their ways, and were resistant to change.

The other thing, of course, was that she had not the faintest idea how to talk to them, how to run a staff meeting, or how to do job assessments or distribute the work. In short, she had never been a boss before and had no training for her new responsibilities.

Later Belinda said it had been the steepest learning curve of her career. "At the time I was so naive, I was really scared to talk to my staff. I was totally incapable of reprimanding anyone, and I think they all knew that. Doing annual work assessments was a nightmare because I was afraid to criticize them in any way.

"I would say that I was a really bad boss; I had no training myself so how could I supervise them in their various jobs? I was looking to them to tell me what they were doing and how they were doing it.

"Sadly, I don't think much has changed in this regard. I see it all the time, with people being promoted or appointed without anyone giving a thought to whether they have any leadership skills or any training in the role. They are appointed because they can do a specific job well—but now they have to do something else: take charge of a section or department. They are not bad people, but too often they go from great individual performer to lousy boss. It's unfair to all parties."

My take: Belinda's story is all too familiar. Millions of bosses have been thrust into similar situations. Unfamiliar with the demands of leadership, naive about its pitfalls and inexperienced in human dynamics, they are set up for failure. As to where the blame lies, it is clearly with senior leaders who casually make such appointments without regard to the consequences. It turns out that one of those is an estimated loss to corporate business of $500 billion annually!

BEGINNING A BEAUTIFUL FRIENDSHIP
By Shel Holtz

Initially, Ed Hahn intimidated me. During my interview with him, and continuing in my first days as employee communication manager at Mattel, I was concerned my new boss would be a stern taskmaster. He reminded me for all the world of Professor Kingsfield from *The Paper Chase*. He had a salt-and-pepper beard, peered at me over reading glasses perched on the end of his nose, and spoke with assured authority.

After a few days of my settling into the job, though, Ed called me into his office to talk about how we would work together. Ed was Director of Organization Development. I reported to him because I had to report somewhere and nobody in the Human Resources department was quite sure where that should be.

"I don't know anything about what you do," he said, "but I trust you to do your job. Report to me every week or two so I know what you're up to and let me know if you need my help."

That was, as Rick said to Captain Louis in the movie *Casablanca*, the beginning of a beautiful friendship that endures to this day. I learned more about being a manager and a leader in business from Ed than all the rest of my bosses combined—including books, classes, TED Talks, and conference sessions.

Ed and I wound up spending a lot of time together. In my office. In his office. In the cafeteria. At a bar and grill a block or two away. At his place in a beach community not far from our office. Rarely did our conversation veer away from management and leadership; they were his passions. He was seriously focused on employee engagement years before it became a thing.

He also guided me in how to build strong relationships with those above me in the hierarchy and often paved the way for those relationships. On more than one occasion, he went to bat for me, supporting something I wanted to do that some leaders didn't understand.

For example, the last of the company's U.S. manufacturing facilities was closing. We interviewed employees about its legacy as a vital part of Mattel's corporate history. The senior VP of Operations initially killed the story. "Why would we want to talk about that?" he asked dismissively. "It's bad news."

My explanations fell on deaf ears, but Ed sat down with him and agreed to let the story run. It was one of the most-read stories we ever produced, most likely because it had a refreshing and honest focus on a legacy rather than what a senior leader could only perceive as "bad news."

My take: The lesson here is trust. Select the right people and trust them to do the job. And then mentor them, as Ed did, to further develop their skills and perspective.

As a development expert at InterContinental Hotels once observed to me, "If you want people who smile and are cordial to guests, hire cordial people who smile, and then teach them the hotel business." It was a piece of wisdom I've never forgotten.

MUTUAL TRUST AND SAFE RISK-TAKING
By Kellie Garrett

A major research study by Google of its highest performing teams revealed that the secret to their success is psychological safety—which enables vulnerability and trust. When employees feel safe, they are willing to risk failure, a key element of innovation and learning.

The best CEO I ever worked for was masterful at creating a safe environment.

John Ryan was CEO of Farm Credit Canada for a decade. He transformed a sleepy federal Crown organization into a financial powerhouse and number five among Canada's top 50 employers. As a newly minted vice president, I was in my dream job, I hadn't aspired to be an executive, but I loved having a seat at the mahogany table.

Within a couple of years of working for him, I took a six-week holiday, and was home for two days between a honeymoon overseas and a canoe trip with my young sons and extended family. John's assistant called me and said that John urgently needed to see me.

I asked if I was in trouble, and she laughed. So I dug up some business duds and went to see my favorite boss.

"I want you to take a two-year assignment," John said. "You'll be VP of Marketing and Product Development, while the incumbent is working on an e-business project."

"That's not a great idea," I protested. "I don't know anything about financial products or call centers, and they're about to develop a customer-relationship management solution. I'm not the right person. Besides, I'm in my dream job."

"You're the most creative person I know," John said. "You will be a breath of fresh air in product development. And you can figure out anything."

"I'm not so sure about that…" John looked at me intently, with a half-smile. "Do you trust me?" His earnestness and warmth disarmed me, as always.

"Of course," I replied, knowing that I was hooked.

I spent the next three weeks paddling through the wilds of Quebec, fretting about how I'd get up to speed quickly on my new duties. I didn't sleep well for three months. I interviewed every employee, pored over business literature, and learned the ins and outs of customer loyalty, product management, and average speed of answer. John was right. I figured it out.

My take: The CEO in this story shows us the value of creating an environment that encourages a reluctant employee to take a risk. If we want people to grow in their careers, we need to provide the reassurance and encouragement that they will be supported in whatever personal risk is involved in their growth.

One of the most basic needs any employee has is captured in the question: Does anyone care about me? In fact, it is one of the primary determinants of whether or not a person will choose to engage, to invest that productivity gift we can freely give or silently withhold without anyone being the wiser.

POLISHING A BOOT
By Dan Koger

I'd like to add a somewhat unusual example of a Good Boss, Shipfitter 1st Class Jerome David Lawson, U.S. Navy. Jerry Lawson was the Company Commander of my recruit company in Navy Boot Camp at Naval Station Great Lakes, on Lake Michigan midway between Chicago and Milwaukee.

I can honestly say that Jerry's leadership kept me from going nuts during an intense period designed to make or break you, under the Navy's not unreasonable theory that if a recruit was going to crack under pressure, better to find that out in a pyrotechnics-free barracks on dry land than in a warship packed with explosives.

I was in Jerry's recruit company during one of the worst winters in Northern Illinois history. My first encounter with Jerry was while I was standing in line, in the civilian clothes I'd been wearing for the past three days, waiting for a snarling barber to cut off all my hair.

"Koger, you a college graduate?" Jerry snapped at me, his face about three inches from mine.

"Yes sir," I replied, standing rigidly at attention.

"You going to screw with me, college boy?" Jerry said.

"No sir, Company Commander," I said.

"That's good. We had some college boys here and they tried to mess with us. Not good," Jerry said, shaking his head, apparently in sorrowful memory of the late-lamented academic interlopers.

As he walked away, Jerry said, "I'll be watching you."

He wasn't kidding. He did watch me and apparently liked what he saw because a few days later he appointed me Master-at-Arms for the company, which meant that I was responsible for the safety and motivational condition of all 85 of my fellow recruits during those long winter periods when we were in our barracks.

Like any good boss, Jerry provided me with clear objectives—keep everyone alive and healthy—and clear criteria for success: don't let anyone break the rules too much, and don't let anyone go AWOL. No fights, and smoking only in designated areas at designated times. Don't let them burn the place down.

I kept the recruits in one piece for the next two months and Jerry rewarded me by recommending me for Officer Candidate School. A bad report from Jerry would have deep-sixed my OCS application. Shipfitter 1st Class Jerome Lawson turned out to be the ideal boss.

My take: The military with its autocratic and hierarchical culture may seem to be the last place to look for a boss model for contemporary workers.

But the military's value system teaches us some important lessons. There is its leadership training with an emphasis on becoming the true servant leader; the officer's first designated responsibility is to take care of their men and women. There's also the constant commitment to training and ongoing performance feedback.

Recognition of solid performance is mandatory and tangibly rewarded with medals, ceremonies, and promotions. Civilian leaders could do worse than emulating those same values.

JACK THE BUFFER
By Shel Holtz

I was hired at a Fortune 500 pharmaceutical company as manager of employee communication, reporting to the VP of HR.

Soon after I joined the business there was a reorganization. I was promoted to corporate director, reporting to a new head of Industrial Relations. This individual, Jack, had worked at a separate business owned on the side by the company's CEO as something of a hobby. In that role he cozied up to the CEO, and that in turn led to a job at the corporation, where he moved up quickly.

For his job as head of Industrial Relations Jack had no experience, no background, and no clue. Other than an administrative assistant, he had never had anybody report to him before.

It's important to understand the role Jack played in the company: he was a buffer between the president and the CEO and the rest of the company. He filtered upward information, making sure the CEO and his senior staff didn't hear anything he didn't want them to hear or that might make him look bad. He completely controlled access to them.

I attempted to develop a media-relations strategy, he rebuffed the effort; my job, he said, was to keep us out of the press. When I refused to follow his instructions to lie to a reporter over a company issue, he fired me.

My take: Self-serving and underqualified bosses wreak havoc on an organization's function and the professionals who staff it by distorting their proper role and taking advantage of favored relationships. When they have support from a corrupt leader, the damage to both a work group and its professionals can be devastating and lasting.

In their insecurity and incompetence, they too often act irrationally and arbitrarily, leaving a lasting mark on the people and functions they mismanage. Worst of all, in misguided efforts to block bad news, they deny senior leaders the information they need to make informed decisions.

UGLY IN HONG KONG
By David Norris

I encountered my first truly "ugly" boss midway through my career. Shortly before his arrival I had drafted a turnaround strategy for our division, challenged by economic and technological change. My boss reviewed it and said that he wouldn't take it further; he had other ideas. But there were some early warning signs, such as the exclusion of subordinates from important emails, his rapid judgment that certain people were not "up to our high standards," or his special deference toward senior management.

On the surface, though, all was well. Management commented favorably on the "energy" and "high impact" this individual brought. He was a hit on the company social circuit, and even started dating the CEO of one of our biggest divisions.

To the immediate team, the reality was less sanguine. Six months into his appointment, we felt lost. Far from improving, we were going backward. Senior management eventually sensed trouble and set a hard deadline for him to develop plans to turn things around. At the last minute before the deadline expired, he finally sent the plan through.

My relief quickly turned to disbelief. The paper seemed oddly familiar. Blinking, I recognized that this was actually the strategy I had created the year before. The only differences were that the headers were now a different color and a few words had been tweaked. The document's properties section even showed my name as the author! It was my plan that he submitted to senior management—all without any prior discussion with the team, including me, the original author.

Over time things got worse. My boss complained that we were letting him down. Recruiters weren't giving us good candidates; staff members weren't pulling their weight; vendors were falling down on their promises; he had to spend time revising poor work. As if to maintain a space of psychological safety, he grew more desperate, even vindictive toward those who saw through him.

I was fortunate to have enough work experience to put all this in perspective. Other team members were less inclined to tolerate the situation. Several quit, as did their replacements, at an alarmingly rapid rate.

One by one, he lost the confidence of subordinates, peers, and finally senior management. Around the end of his third year, he was invited to leave the company.

My take: David's summing up captures the lesson perfectly. "This experience was new: the first time I'd had a manager who was both incompetent in their craft and damaging in their style. Looking back, it makes me reflect on how much of an impact a boss can have. The experience deepened my conviction that companies must recruit well and, post-appointment, be alert for early warning signs and prepared to act on them swiftly."

Why Things Go Wrong

One reason for the inattention to leadership roles is sheer hierarchical distance and perhaps the faith that bosses do the best they can, given the role's demands.

Seeing that role as narrowly supervisory in accomplishing job tasks may also be a factor. In truth, there are likely as many reasons as there are types and styles of senior leaders. One has to presume that if senior leaders actually recognized the costs in disengagement, excessive turnover and mismanagement of talent they would be sufficiently aroused to address the issue with the urgency it demands.

As for picking the wrong candidate 82 percent of the time, this is simply a failure to establish success criteria and install a rigorous selection process.

I am appalled at how little thought is sometimes given to major leadership appointments or promotions. I have been a witness on a number of occasions to senior leaders casually making important appointments with a dismissive, "Send her over to Pete; he'll straighten her out" followed by a satisfied "Done."

The neglect results in choices being based not on sound deliberation but instead on favoritism, gender and/or racial bias, and promotion of people who may have been great individual contributors but who turn out to be obsessive micromanagers. All these factors are high on the list of reasons for poor candidate selection.

Another failure in boss development is not providing well-considered, well-delivered leadership training. Recall that the ROI Communication study quoted earlier shows that only 33 percent of bosses get *any* training for the job.

Training is expensive and labor intensive when done right. Since the costs of *not* training are usually hidden opportunity costs, it's an easy line item to delete at budget time. Also the return on investment is rarely clear-cut, making broad-based training hard to rationalize to a skeptical CEO.

A much more subtle problem that goes mostly unrecognized is the nasty reality of staff silos and accompanying turf issues.

Here's a personal example from three different and highly regarded Fortune 500 companies. The first was a cable provider, the second was a pharmaceutical company, and the third was a chemical company.

Over an extended period, our team of consultants had worked with our clients' staff professionals to design and deliver tailored communication-training initiatives for new and current company bosses. When such projects involve two separate functions—in this case HR and Communication—the turf issues can become dicey.

In all three cases, the client's staff professionals collaborated with us to make the business case justifying the initiative. From that business case, we partnered to ensure the initiatives were well grounded and responsive to the differing company needs.

When it came time to win final approval to implement the initiatives, the HR vice president inexplicably raised a host of questions and challenges. Something was obviously amiss. What became clear finally was that despite our warnings, our HR partners had neglected to keep their own functional leaders informed and on board.

The deal-breaking issue was who should deliver the training—the communication subject-matter experts or the HR professional trainers. Suddenly aroused about their turf interests and who should deliver the training, both the HR and the Communication VP's refused to budge and quietly abandoned the training initiatives.

It was the same basic story in all three companies: last-minute, alleged second thoughts about the wisdom and efficacy of the training, masking what were really turf rivalries.

Needless to say, the three initiatives never saw the light of day because of the turf wrangling. No question that turf fights at the senior-staff level cost organizations millions of dollars in wasted time and intellectual energy, not to mention lost opportunities. In this case, badly needed communication leadership training.

Dysfunctional Cultures

Another cause that often undermines proper boss development is dysfunctional organizational cultures.

Bosses are particularly adept at reading the actual versus the idealized corporate culture in which they operate, learning where the boundaries are, what is likely to be rewarded, and what could well lead to trouble and career-limiting consequences.

The next stories illustrate what happens when cultures go awry, leading to executive shenanigans and worse.

CUISINER LES LIVRES À LA VINDALOO
(Or "Cooking the Books Vindaloo Style")
By Bish Mukherjee

"KK" and I joined the company on the same day, he as the Finance Head and I as the Communications Head in New Delhi. We jelled together well and became buddies at work. We shared each other's interests and strategies and supported each other as best we could.

We were both reporting to the Chairman, though I had a dotted-line reporting relationship to KK as well.

The three of us did some pioneering work during the splitting of the parent Anglo-French multinational company into two parts. We helped with the setting up of the new French company that was then listed in New York, London, and Paris.

Our Chairman was under intense pressure to show profits from the India company when there were none. So he began selling off some of the company's so-called "dead" assets and doing some "book-cooking" of the company's accounts at the behest of KK.

KK, as the Head of Finance, was privy to the situation. But it was kept a secret from the parent company. During one of his visits to Paris, KK met with the global Finance Head and informed him of the Chairman's actions. After he returned to New Delhi, KK was asked by the global Finance Head to keep him posted of every such asset-selling move.

The Paris company prepared a detailed case against the Chairman over the next few months, presented it to the board, and compelled the Chairman, who never suspected KK's role, to quit the company.

Later I found out from my French colleagues that KK had convinced management in Paris that he should be made the Managing Director (CEO) of the India company. The French company did exactly that and brought in a non-Executive Director as the new Chairman and named KK as the new Managing Director of Indian operations.

But the icing on the cake came when, after taking charge of the India operations, KK justified selling of assets as the only way for the company to survive. So he did exactly the same thing, conspiring behind his own boss's back and getting him removed! KK remained at the helm in India for a couple of years and then he managed to get posted to Paris. He never returned to live in India.

My take: Corporate chicanery is far from unknown, but when a financial manager urges a sell-off of non-performing assets, collaborates in a cover-up, orchestrates a "cooking" of company books, gets his boss fired, and then lobbies to succeed him, the treachery is reminiscent of the twists and turns of one of Will Shakespeare's tragedies.

Hiding in the Weeds

In rare cases an entire company can exhibit signs of dysfunction. Two vivid examples come to mind.

One was a Canadian company that undertook a downsizing in which management decided to move quickly with what they considered the least disruption—sort of like ripping off a Band-Aid in one swift motion.

It was an oil sands company operating in the Canadian frontier country near Fort McMurray. The company head called an all-employee meeting in which the attendees were given color-coded cards that sent them to designated breakout groups. One led to actual meetings.

The other led to a room in which employees heard that they had been selected for a reduction in force. Counselors were present to help them absorb the news and counsel them in finding other employment. Company leaders apparently believed this was a humane and orderly way to conduct a downsizing.

But the participants learned the true reality of the company culture on that noteworthy day.

The other case was a region of a major U.S. railroad known for its contentious relations with its union. Like the oil sands case, the tactic was to call an all-employee regional meeting at a designated company venue.

Shortly after the people arrived, all of the doors were locked and security proceeded to conduct "a shake-down inspection" and a drug bust complete with urine tests all around.

The action could be rationalized as a means of protecting the public from unsafe employees. But the problem was the use of deceptive means leading to a severe hangover of mistrust.

The following excerpt of an anonymous post on the well-visited Glassdoor website shows that the drug bust was not an isolated incident:

"Working for this railroad is great if you like being bullwhipped. Bosses have a quota to fire so many people per month, so they hide in the weeds with binoculars trying to find you doing something against the rules. God forbid you get injured; they'll fire you.

"I have seen people hurt badly and too scared to turn it in for fear of losing their job. They fire you for breaking a rule but often tell you to do something against the rules. It's all good as long as it helps them. It is a horrible place to work, long hours away from family, holidays missed, birthdays, everything missed, they do not care. Think hard before hiring on, if you're married you will get divorced, if you're not married you never will be. Home is wherever they tell you.

"So pack your bags. Managers are so dumb, you know the ones that fire you by quota. Most of them got their jobs by being injured and accepting a management position and money for not suing. Now with Trump in office I'm sure the railroad can get away with whatever they want to. And believe me, it won't be good for the employee."

Some of that may well be a disaffected employee's exaggeration, but the post's damage to company reputation is irreversible.

And there you have it: some enlightened leadership practices, but widespread development neglect of bosses by senior leaders, poor selection practices in the first place, silo rivalries, naiveté about workable solutions, rogue cultures, and even violation of fiduciary responsibility.

Let's look next at the "top dogs" in organizations and their critical role as models of good or bad leadership behavior.

TOP DOGS

So far the stories reported here by the panelists have mostly focused on the behavior of middle and lower-level bosses, which begs the question of what about the Top Dogs in organizations? These are the people who supposedly make the big decisions, not to mention receive the big compensation. In the rest of this chapter we'll look at two questions:

- What are the essential qualities that enable a CEO (or other senior executive) to create and maintain a safe culture where innovation and creativity are the competitive difference?
- Who are credible examples of such behavior?

As far as the qualities needed to be such a senior executive, they are both basic and rare. The first is obviously integrity, the resolve to do the right thing regardless of the cost, personal or otherwise. Most of the others flow from that basic quality.

A person of demonstrated integrity typically engenders the trust of followers. Those two qualities—integrity in word and action, and trust earned over time—are essential to real leadership. A strong inclination to kindness and respect for another's dignity also doesn't hurt.

But in Ugly Boss circles, that's seen as weakness. In the best places to work, it's seen as routine. And finally, the willingness to tell and to listen to the unvarnished truth in an open and transparent manner is the essential enabler of a safe culture.

When I was a young man working for General Electric in the early 1960s, there was a clear company leadership credo that said that GE had four primary and equivalent audiences: customers, shareholders, the communities in which they did business, and employees. This was no hierarchy. These audiences had parity that must be respected. In the intervening years in companies in general, two of the audiences—employees and communities—have been relegated to a lesser status. Shareholders, on the other hand, have received the lion's share of senior-leader attention in the name of "increasing shareholder value," not to mention their own personal stake in overseeing a rising share price.

In his excellent 2018 book *Temp: How American Work, American Business, and the American Dream Became Temporary*, historian Louis Hyman blames the influence of management consultants on CEOs and other senior leaders for reinventing work and the mission of business. He also charges that companies became more inhospitable employers by turning work into something robots could do cheaper and more efficiently.

To compete, he asserts, employees themselves had to become human machines who accept long hours, don't join unions, are willing to work any shift, and are easy to hire and equally easy to fire. In Hyman's words, "the key features of the postwar corporations—stable workforces, retained earnings and minimized risk—became liabilities rather than assets."

Historian Jill Lepore, in the March 4, 2019 *New Yorker* article entitled "The Robot Caravan" adds, "If businesses exist not to make things and employ people but instead to maximize profits for investors, labor can be done by temps, by poorly paid workers in other countries, or by robots, whichever is cheapest."

In her comment, she neatly sums up the dilemma that has faced us for the last 40 years, beginning in the 1980s when corporate leadership determined that they must become "lean" in order to maximize earnings and shareholder value. The change in mission and business philosophy is profound.

Another crucial reason for the neglect of both employees and their communities is global competition and the perceived need to be the lowest-cost producer to compete. As for the communities, the work was sent to those places with the cheapest labor costs—typically another country than the United States with lower standards of living and a population eager for any kind of work. As a result, both those communities and their residents paid a price. A train ride through just about any major U.S. city will reveal a backdrop of abandoned factories, graffiti-marked with their windows shattered by unknown passers-by. Buildings that once housed thriving manufacturing businesses.

Employees took a double whammy in job loss and having to live in newly destabilized communities. They became the mechanism, through downsizing and mergers, to help inflate profits while most investors looked on, largely indifferent to their plight.

You need only look at the positive reaction of the investment community at almost every major downsizing or anticipated merger to see this. If share prices increase, a search for "duplication of resources and people" is inevitably undertaken to further increase shareholder return.

In the ensuing disruption too many leaders neglect the talent base of their companies. Bosses are left to their own interpretations, clearly observing the real values of their leaders, and passing them on to team members.

Is it any wonder that many of these same bosses replicate the behavior they observe at the top? Perhaps the wonder is that so many of them choose to be as humane and enlightened as they can within the constraints of the day.

Fundamental Employee Information Needs

For their part employees have essentially three crucial questions they want answered in the face of today's workplace change. If you're looking for an employee communication strategy, address these three questions as your starting point:

- Where are we going as an organization?
- How do we propose to get there?
- And then the most important of all: what does this mean to/for *me*?

The safest bet one can make is that the criticism leveled by Louis Hyman and Jill Lepore will continue to describe the state of global business. That means that many workers are pretty much on their own in managing their work lives. In turn, the three questions posed above take on a new urgency. These employees are subject to the whiplash of change leading to insecurity and the constant fear of job loss. Under those circumstances, it's incumbent on leaders to provide information that will permit them to truly size up their job prospects and to make decisions about their futures

Going forward senior leaders have the responsibility not only to keep employees well-informed but also to lead in such a way that takes their welfare into account. A looming example is artificial intelligence (AI) and its capacity to further undermine job security by enabling greater automation.

When I was a young professional at GE in the 1960s, I vividly recall reading a company handout that sought to reassure union employees about the onset of automation. The basic message was: "Don't worry. Automation will create many more jobs than it will ever destroy." I was somewhat skeptical at the time. Today I'm even more so.

At the 2019 Davos economic conference one of the main topics of conversation was the race to automate work and reduce the workforce. *New York Times* reporter Kevin Roose put it in these stark terms in a January 25, 2019 article entitled "The Hidden Automation Agenda of the Davos Elite."

"All over the world, executives are spending billions of dollars to transform their businesses into lean, digitized, highly automated operations. They crave the fat profit margins automation can deliver, and they see AI as a golden ticket to savings, perhaps by letting them whittle departments with thousands of workers down to just a few dozen."

Later in the same report, Roose quotes Kai-Fu Lee, the author of *AI Superpowers* and a longtime technology executive, as predicting "artificial intelligence will eliminate 40 percent of today's jobs within 15 years."

Note, however, that Roose also quotes other experts who predict that AI will probably create more jobs than it destroys and that it will free workers to focus on creative tasks over routine ones.

In the same Times article, Ben Pring, the Director of the Center for the Future of Work, is quoted on the crucial issue of the loss of existing jobs.

"That's the great dichotomy. On one hand, profit-minded executives absolutely want to automate as much as they can. On the other hand, they're facing a backlash in civic society."

Consultants McKinsey & Company in their public statements take up this challenge and are advising clients to mount an integrated digital-transformation strategy at all deliberate speed. They advise allaying any fears and uneasiness executives may harbor, including loss of their own positions, as they move forward with AI. What they most warn against is "incrementalism."

Whichever way this emerging strategy unfolds, it is still one more challenge to senior leaders and employees as they attempt to prepare for the future. Let's hope that the so-called "civic" or social issues get a full and sensitive hearing in the AI debate.

Much is at stake, and it needs transparency to the public given the unknowns. One can only hope that all parties finally create solutions that are in the interests of society at large and not merely to the advantage of a privileged, wealthy few. Both the future intended and unintended consequences loom large.

Good Dog

There are no easy solutions, but one thing is clear: we need to do some hard thinking about what it means to be a good leader in today's environment.

In a day when innovation and creativity are vital competitive weapons, it's essential to create an environment in which people can try out ideas without fear of being harshly judged or having ideas abruptly dismissed.

Here are a couple of stories that make the point that leadership style strongly influences people's willingness to take risks in telling truth to power. Pat Kelly, the senior executive who headed a $24 billion-a-year unit of Pfizer, the world's largest pharmaceutical company, is the focus of the first. His former speechwriter, a position that inevitably gives the writer a close-up look at the boss—warts and all, relates the stories.

TWO LEADERS DELIVER LESSONS FOR A LIFETIME
By Robert Libbey

After months of a successful working relationship as Pat Kelly's speechwriter, I suffered the first setback. It came in four words handwritten in the right margin of a draft of a major speech he was to give in a week or so: "We can do better."

Only "See me" might have been worse. Coming from a person whom I had quickly grown to know as a voluble storyteller on almost any topic, the message could not have been more pointed.

Speechwriting is a tenuous profession, with high-leverage encounters daily. In the best of arrangements, the writer works directly with the speaker. That's best for the final product, but it also means that when you miss in the drafting process or anywhere along the way, that miscue is seen and judged by the leader of the entire organization.

Worse, if a finished speech falls flat—or, and this is nearly unthinkable for the writer and speaker alike, there is a factual error in the text—it's all on you.

As a result, the draft-and-review process can feel like a merry-go-round of never-ending performance reviews, at least until you establish a solid relationship with the speaker.

There is no getting around this vulnerability. The highs of a successful address feel ethereal, but the lows scrape and grind the very underbody of professional experience. This explains why many speechwriters seem to work in a state of chronic uncertainty that they try to cover with whatever real confidence they have and sometimes a little false bravado as a cushion.

Back to the keyboard.

Once I shook off the initial impact of those four words ("We can do better") I sat back in my small midtown Manhattan office and re-read the draft. A couple of days removed from its completion, the specific problems the boss had caught were clear to me. I wrote my edits onto the hard copy of the draft, went back to the keyboard and made the changes.

Since there were only two offices between us, I knew I'd have a chance to mention to him that day or the next that I had a new draft for review. And that's just what we did, later that same day.

We sat in his corner office overlooking East 42nd Street and read through the piece together; or, as usual, he read and made a few more marks to the text, while I waited and scanned the pages of my copy. After 20 minutes—or a little longer than the address would last—he was finished and declared it good, with a smile and a few words of thanks for responding quickly.

Relief. We were back on track, and I would enjoy one of the most productive and satisfying partnerships of my career.

What made that alliance so productive and satisfying? First, Pat Kelly was especially intelligent, had a wide-ranging understanding of both the big issues of the day and the latest cultural totems, and was a skilled writer himself. This made him tough to keep up with, as is the case with most senior executives; but his thinking was always interesting.

Second, he was generally willing to take risks. Together, all of this meant that he invariably made my work better. (It certainly helped that earlier in his career he was doing much the same work I was.) He also had a great sense of humor that was equaled by his feel for people and his audience. He was generous in his feedback and appreciative of a job well done.

He wasn't my direct manager—that was another staff member who reported to Pat—but he was my boss in the sense that almost all work was for him, and my success in the company depended on his assessment of that work.

Two other characteristics made him a great boss.

The first was his ability to communicate and, in the process, to teach. "We can do better." This was the clearest feedback I had ever received. It was brief, simple, and direct. There was no room for misunderstanding. If feedback is the light that illuminates our path to improvement, this marked very clearly for me the best way to provide it and a standard that I work to reach consistently.

The second characteristic that distinguished Pat Kelly as a great boss was his commitment to pushing the envelope to make a good idea better. He did this often with me and I saw him do it regularly with others. In pushing us to produce at a higher level, he set a clear example for the entire organization.

AN UNFLAPPABLE LEADER
By Robert Libbey

The second great boss in my career was also a top executive—Jim Orr, CEO of insurance company Unum. He was a terrific leader and very good speaker who taught me two important lessons, among others. I worked with him for a decade earlier in my career. While he was different from Pat Kelly in style, he was equally instructive in collaborating, generous, and thoroughly unflappable.

On one memorable occasion, Jim gave a speech that was marred in its opening by sound system problems. It was one of the first major speeches we worked on together. I was standing in the back of the room, as I usually did, and a UNUM senior executive stood by me. At the conclusion of the speech, the nearby exec whispered to me: "I don't think he was very good." I didn't agree.

I sensed that Jim wasn't as sure as I was about his performance when, after walking back from the podium, he asked me how I thought it had gone.

I told him directly what I thought he did well and made a couple of small suggestions for the future. He didn't seem entirely convinced. So, taking a different tack, I took a chance and added: "Well, either way, I don't think you said anything that's going to send the stock down four points."

He looked at me, broke into a smile and said, "Good, but it wouldn't be the first time if I had."

With that wind at my back, I thought it important to let him know that one of his senior people didn't share my sentiment. Again, he smiled, and then said: "Don't worry about that kind of stuff. You're always going to get some of that."

Here was a young CEO—in his early-to-mid-40s at the time—who had just completed an important speech under trying circumstances taking the time to share his advice with a mid-level staffer. That alone struck me as both unusual and generous. "Don't let the inevitable negative opinions of others trip you up."

His focus on others came through later in our time together, when I was pushing (respectfully) for him to take a position on an issue in the company that I thought was fully within his rights as CEO. He listened, acknowledged the idea, and then said to me, and I paraphrase: "I'm only in this job for now. There were plenty who came before me and more will follow."

In other words, he saw his position as that of a servant to the company's many constituencies, not one that he defined or one that defined him.

Years later, someone else did take that role, following a so-called merger of equals that turned ugly with accusations about the strength of the company's core business. In the end that accusation turned out to be truer about the new partner's business. Through it all, Jim Orr never publicly said a bad word about anyone involved and I never heard him make such comments privately.

The lessons that Jim Orr and Pat Kelly imparted have endured long beyond the moment and this, perhaps more than anything, is what makes a great boss great.

My take: These stories share two themes. First is the humanity of both leaders and their ability to create that safe environment so necessary to risk-taking and solid performance. And second is their commitment to honest feedback and the creation of trust.

Most of us are sensitive to harsh criticism so any boss providing critical feedback is walking on eggshells. It's important to be gentle and respectful when one is attempting to identify a problem and deal with it. Pat Kelly knew that so his words were candid and encouraging rather than dispiriting. "We can do better." Note the use of "we" and the implication that together we can solve this issue. Here's a contrasting example.

CARLY THE CORPORATE ROCK STAR
By Priya Bates

I worked for Compaq Canada after and before the Hewlett Packard (HP)/Compaq merger and had the privilege of working on the global integration team for the merger itself.

In that capacity, I got to watch the new CEO, Carly Fiorina, from afar and sometimes up close. It was wonderful to have a female leader who was receiving global recognition.

Carly was a visionary who recognized the need for change in HP—an organization that she said often was suffering from "analysis paralysis" and increased bureaucracy. Having briefed Carly for Canadian presentations on several occasions, I was completely in awe of her stage presence and ability to bring a briefing to life in mere minutes.

In my experience the best leaders understand what they are good at and where they add value and surround themselves with complementary leaders who can fill in the gaps and lead in their areas of expertise.

Carly's biggest flaw was craving the spotlight and believing she could do it all herself. She loved being on stage as the center of attention. Her ideas and vision were sound, but she lacked the ability to operationalize the dream—the real day-to-day stuff that converts dreams into realities.

Culturally, HP and Compaq came together quite successfully. As employees we bought into the vision, but as time went on, we clearly weren't headed in the right direction. Carly Fiorina was let go in 2005 amidst differences with the Board of Directors. In 2005. At the time of her firing, a *Wall Street Journal* described her as the epitome of "an alluring, controversial new breed of chief executive officer, who combine grand visions with charismatic but self-centered and demanding styles."

The same year, Wharton School professor Michael Useem (an interestingly named gentleman given his assessment of Fiorina's performance) opined: "Fiorina scored high on leadership style, but she failed to execute strategy." However much as employees were initially enamored with Carly and enjoyed seeing her on stage, the disconnect between her vision and HP performance signaled again that performance wins every time.

My take: Carly is not alone in her failure as CEO in trying to turn a vision, which by its very nature is aspirational, into a workable strategy. Aside from the internal resistance to change, there is the uphill effort to communicate a message of major change to a large employee audience. It takes backbone and persistence to stay the course.

Unfortunately, too many senior leaders lack the stamina to pull it off. Just about the umpteenth time the message is "gagging the leader" is about when it is beginning to get through to the audience. Creative repetition is mandatory.

This next story shows the challenge of delivering an important message to a hard-working and hard-driving team leader.

A "NICE" COACH
By Stacy Wilson

The best boss I ever worked for was at Sprint PCS. Ed Mattix empowered his team members to do great work every day. He gave us resources, freedom, and his support. He hired people who knew things he didn't, and he served as a sounding board when we needed to think collaboratively.

One day Ed called me into his office. I recall being nervous as I made my way there. I also recall sitting at the conference table in his office, where we'd celebrated his birthday with phone calls from a handful of his favorite NFL players.

He told me I was doing a great job. I sensed a "but" coming. "Could you just be a little nicer," he said smiling.

I never expected more from my staff than I did from myself. But at the time, I was a driven workaholic. Someone on my team had expressed concern about my unyielding attitude and tone. Ed did a great job bringing this up in a way that incorporated humor and compassion.

I was nervous as I made my way there. I recall sitting at the conference table in his office, where we'd celebrated his birthday with phone calls from a handful of his favorite NFL players.

He told me I was doing a great job. I sensed a "but" coming. "Could you just be a little nicer," he said smiling.

I never expected more from my staff than I did from myself. But, at the time, I was a driven workaholic. Someone on my team had expressed concern about my unyielding attitude and tone. Ed did a great job bringing this up in a way that incorporated humor and compassion.

It stuck with me. I believe I, like other women, demonstrated too hard an edge to make up for perceived gender gaps. To this day, I still check myself with that statement. Might softening my approach pave the way for success? It was a simple, but brilliant, lesson for leadership coaching.

My take: One of the hardest challenges a boss faces is finding balance in relationships with team members. Ed delivered a potentially painful message with humor and grace, a talent that requires excellent human relations skills. It's likely the reason that only 10 to 20 percent of us have what it takes to lead.

The Sum of Its Parts

Fine, you might say, if you're lucky enough to work for people like this, but what about a company as a whole? Does enlightened behavior at the top ensure that other bosses will behave in similar fashion? The obvious answer is, at best, maybe. Role modeling at the top can be very powerful, but not always.

What's needed is a deliberate initiative with a solid strategy, and most of all, accountability for the behavior bosses need to display. Without that accountability, any initiative in this direction is merely a suggestion that people can take or leave.

Here's an example of an initiative that includes all of the touch points—a strategy, proper modeling, and training and accountability. Once again our exemplar is Pfizer. In 2012 Pfizer's leadership launched a five-part initiative entitled Creating an Ownership Culture abbreviated simply to the acronym OWNIT!

The five parts of the initiative were based on the meaning of that acronym.

"O" stood for Own the business, meaning to seize opportunities to think differently and be accountable.

"W" was for win in the marketplace, translated to supporting long-term and aligned strategies.

"N" was the most daring part of the initiative in my opinion. It stood for "No jerks" and referred to boss behavior with the further admonition that there be no corrosive, self-serving, or mean boss behavior. The goal was for the company to be people-oriented as a prime cultural value.

"I" stood for impacting results, delivering on commitments with integrity.

And "T" was for the all-important value of trust in one another and in company relationships. To launch the initiative Pfizer shut down the company for an entire day with employee sessions aimed at explaining and illustrating what OWNIT! truly meant.

Now all of that could have simply ended as a cheerleading exercise if there were no strategy behind it. Instead, a comprehensive manager training and development program was put in place to ensure that the OWNIT! message was understood and taken seriously and that the words and actions matched. The emphasis was on defining results, setting expectations, engaging and building talent, and shaping the company's future. The ultimate goal was to engage everyone in creating that Pfizer ownership culture that would facilitate Pfizer's safe navigation of the challenges inherent in an emerging talent-based culture.

Given the degree of employee skepticism regarding such senior leadership initiatives, it's fair to ask if things like OWNIT! are well received and if they truly make an impact. The honest answer is that their success depends on the credibility of the management team and whether employees perceive that the effort will be supported by appropriate action.

As soon as they intuit the slightest bit of leadership insincerity or manipulation, or worse, actions that contradict the authenticity of the message, employee belief turns to cynicism.

Here is one final example to help make the point. It is QVC, the flagship shopping channel owned by the Qurate Retail Group. Under the leadership of Mike George, CEO and President, the company has engaged in a long-standing initiative to educate employees fully to vision, mission, and strategy.

Much of the initiative comes from George's determination to build what he terms "a culture of leadership" in the company. The fundamental notion is that everyone in QVC must be a leader, with leaders of leaders at the top of the organization, leaders of people in the middle, and "leaders of oneself" as the primary agent and talent in serving customer needs.

QVC's leadership competency model features two foundational leadership behaviors—first to build real customer and colleague relationships and second to lead with agility, all in service to the QVC customer and to colleagues in four crucial tasks. Those four are building the organization's capability by developing talent, helping to shape and define the company's future, engaging and developing teams, and delivering excellent results.

George is relentless in focusing the organization on this leadership culture to the point that he holds all-employee weekly meetings that are both live at headquarters and televised to other geographic locations. The entire culture of leadership initiative is fully supported by Human Resources and other staff functions to keep the company focused on necessary changes.

Once again, how successful will such company initiatives be in the long run? That will depend on how seriously people are held accountable as companies actualize their talent base. In the end, long-term success will depend too on serious leadership at all levels, but especially at the first-line boss level, where the most important interaction takes place.

A truly skeptical boss can undo the best of such strategies with a knowing wink or a nod. The lesson is that senior leaders better include and inform them and then demonstrate honest intention through action.

THE REMEDY

I have always wondered why we search for the most talented and qualified candidates we can find for a given job and then immerse them into a system and culture seemingly designed to limit, undermine, inhibit, and discourage their best contributions.

You may well perceive that as an unfair generalization, but look back at some of the experiences reported by the panelists. Or think about your own careers and the times you have been prevented from doing your best work, whatever the cause. Today, more than 200 years after the beginning of industrialization we are still struggling with the question of how best to lead human talent.

Some historians argue that we have now entered the fourth iteration of an ongoing Industrial Revolution. The roots of that revolution can be traced back to the late 1700s and the invention of the steam engine, which finally provided humankind with a source of energy not related to human or animal labor.

This one invention revolutionized industry and led to untold numbers of laborsaving inventions. It also enabled new modes of transportation—most notably the railroads that crisscrossed the country and led to heretofore unheard of growth and mobility.

The Second Industrial Revolution, say the historians, was the invention of turbines capable of converting other power sources, like cascading water and coal, to produce electricity. The possibilities for its use as both industrial and domestic power were practically infinite.

And so this revolution led to everything from lighting the darkness to the manufacture of the devices that enriched our lives and freed us from routine tasks now doable with the flip of a switch. That revolution lasted for almost a century until we saw the early beginnings of the Third Industrial Revolution, with the invention of the first digital devices in the late 1960s. Much of this development was driven by space and military applications that paved the way for an explosion of technology and its derivative commercial products.

The Fourth Industrial Revolution is in its infancy now with gigantic advances like 3-D printing, robotics, and AI, which will allow robots to "think" and "create."

Where that frontier leads us no one can say for sure. But the ultimate story in these four iterations is the need for endless innovation and creativity with all of its expected and unanticipated consequences.

Talent and Technology

We are now faced with the challenge of how to match the development and application of human talent to the technological forces we have unleashed. That challenge is not new, having come with each iteration of our four revolutions.

The steam engine prolonged slavery in the South with the cotton gin and its ability to expand the cotton trade. Electricity made possible the industrial age and the end of the agrarian society. It also hastened the movement of the population from farms to crowded cities and to factories with the relentless exploitation of human labor.

Digital technology has now connected us as never before but has paradoxically distanced us from more personal human connections and practically destroyed our privacy in the bargain. And AI may well lead to intense competition between automation and robots on the one hand and the human need for meaningful work on the other.

Needed: A Radical Shift

So what's the remedy in this contest between our need to create and find meaning in our work and the potential loss of so many of today's jobs? The ultimate solution has to do with the rebalancing of corporate priorities and difficult structural change.

But that solution bumps up against the prevailing proposition that a CEO's primary job is to maximize shareholder value.

The highly influential economist Milton Friedman was the leading author of the idea that shareholders were corporate owners who deserved the lion's share of corporate profits. That pursuit of shareholder value is the one goal that has dominated senior-leader behavior for the last three decades or more.

For example, a Duke University study in 2006 found that 78 percent of public company CEOs said that they would sacrifice long-term economic value for a short-term increase in share price. At a time when CEO compensation and tenure are frequently based on quarterly earnings, there is little surprise in their finding.

One of the simplest and most commonly used strategies to maximize short-term earnings is the reduction or outright elimination of the human component of production. Which obviously does not bode well for today's job holders.

The issue has many self-interested owners: senior leaders who are rewarded to maximize earnings, shareholders who have been conditioned to expect an ever-soaring stock market, customers who want the lowest prices for their purchases and politicians who would rather not think about it.

In the 1970's and '80s when companies first began to ship manufacturing jobs to lower-wage countries, few people were that alarmed. The response was like, "Well, workers can be retrained to do other types of work. There are lots of service jobs available."

Once when I tried that line on a middle-aged woman, who was a GM assembly-line worker, her reply was memorable. "I dropped out of school because I was a poor student. My whole family has worked at this plant for three generations. You want me to get retrained to go to work at Walmart's for a fraction of what I make here? And what about my kids? When this plant closes, where will they go to work?"

I still have no answer to what for her was far from a rhetorical question.

Perhaps the first thing we need to do is get rid of the fiction that shareholders are absentee owners entitled to the lion's share of our enterprise and that they only have the best interests of the organizations they 'own' as paramount. In truth, investors are more like racetrack touts betting on their favorite corporate horse than they are dedicated owners.

For example, in 1950 a typical shareholder held their stock for eight years. Since 2006, the average share has been held for less than a year, according to a December 22, 2019 New York Times Opinion piece published by Stanford professors Ryan Beck and Amit Seru. The enabling culprit is technology-trading, permitting investors to place their bets at will. Together with hedge-fund managers seeking short-term profit, they have altered the fundamentals of capital investment.

The old image of the shareholder as benevolent-owner interested mainly in a fair return on their investments is an anachronism. When CEO stock and bonus compensation are tied to short-term revenue and profit demands, the end game is to strangle the goose and scramble the golden egg.

A straw in the wind that a new perspective is emerging in the corporate world is a 2019 pronouncement of the Business Roundtable. The BRT, an association of CEOs whose mission is to promote the U.S. economy through sound governance policy, has issued a manifesto challenging the view that corporations exist primarily to serve shareholders.

To understand the ramifications of this shift, consider that the same group from the 1990s forward was the chief proponent of a totally opposite position. As endorsers of shareholder primacy, they influenced at least three decades of C-suite determination mainly to enrich shareholders and themselves.

After the admission that the proper role of the corporation is 'to meet the needs of *all* of its stakeholders,' the BRT statement goes on to acknowledge these five leadership obligations:

- Delivering value to customers.
- Investing in employees' skills, inclusion and dignity.
- Dealing fairly with suppliers.

- Supporting company communities.
- Generating long-term value.

Shades of my GE bosses in the 1960s!

And nearly 200 top executives from such companies as Apple, Facebook, Blackrock, Walmart, and Amazon endorsed the declaration.

One outcome in the rebalancing of corporate constituencies' interests may be the recognition finally that we as humans require meaningful work, not just to pay the bills, but fully as important to exercise our need for accomplishment and fulfillment. When that happens, both the organization and we benefit from the resulting creativity and innovation.

Significantly, the group noted in their statement that it believed that "Americans deserve an economy that allows each person to succeed through hard work and creativity and lead a life of meaning and dignity."

Consider by way of contrast that from 1978 to 2018, CEO compensation rose 940% while the average worker wage rose 12% and the S&P 500 rose over 700%. This is according to a study by the Economic Policy Institute.

Besides recognizing the value of work and workers, the manifesto emphasizes the needs of both customers and communities when addressing relentless change. That should be the golden mean by which we measure organizational decisions and priorities.

But it is also a philosophical and moral challenge of awesome dimensions in a society that has proven itself addicted to technology and meritocracy and mostly indifferent to the suffering of the marginalized and impoverished. No question that it will require a radical shift in corporate thinking and leadership strategy.

And it will also require a deliberate leadership initiative and perhaps even the abandonment of the values of raw competition versus collaboration, profit and wealth for the few at the expense of the many and the sanctification of work as a primary human right.

What does all this have to do with good, bad or ugly bosses? The answer lies in the organization's reward system and the behavior that it promotes. Bosses are like the end skater on a whip-lash maneuver, responding to the forces that propel the line. All of the pressures that are generated by what's rewarded in corporate culture affect their actions and support or distort their behavior.

Not to be rapturous about it, but it is in work that we tend to find meaning, self-worth and a sense of our human dignity. To achieve that lofty state we must first understand why work is so important to our well-being. Making the large assumption that rebalancing of corporate priorities is sincere and successfully implemented over time, we must understand and embrace the needs of people in the workplace, and we must raise up leaders who appreciate and address those needs.

What are they? Actually, they're quite simple.

First, as workers, we need to understand expectations and the connection between our work and the goals and success of an enterprise. Without that clarity, we have great difficulty recognizing the meaning of our work. What are we trying to achieve together, and why is it important to do it in the first place? How does my contribution affect the whole, and why should I care? In short, what's my job, and in what ways does my contribution matter?

A second simple worker need is reinforcement of their performance. It's the basic questions we all want answered: Am I performing to expectations? Am I succeeding? And if not, what must I do to adjust my performance? We call the answer to the question How am I doing? by the simple term "feedback." It's the kind of coaching we all need if we are to achieve a level of confidence, job satisfaction, and personal security.

Of these fundamental needs at work, none is more important than recognition for a job well done. That recognition reinforces our self-worth and inclines us to seek more of it. In all my years of consulting, the one lament I've always heard is that "no one ever says thank you for a job well done. You hear about the shortfalls and the mistakes, but rarely does anyone offer praise."

As a panelist reported, one boss summed it all up with the idea that "you need to keep people guessing and a bit off balance. If you praise someone, they'll ease up and stop trying to please you." Actually, that's contrary to everything we know about human motivation. The keep 'em guessing school of non-recognition is dead wrong. People and their work need to be valued. The question is: Does anyone care?

Another thing we know for sure is that humans tend to be social animals who seek like-minded company. That urge is the reason that people love to be part of a well-functioning team. The first connection any employee makes is at the team level, once they have achieved a level of comfortable and confident personal performance.

It's the easiest connection to make because people are connecting with people they have come to know and, in the best cases, trust. It is a level of intimacy that can only be achieved within a small group and with an enlightened boss.

If people experience ongoing satisfaction of those three 'I needs,' then there is a magic that happens in their thinking and actions. At that point they are able to move beyond 'I needs' to 'we needs.' Bosses need to learn to listen for that powerful transition when the pronoun 'we' becomes common team-usage. If it doesn't happen, it is unlikely that a work group will become a true team. A vital part of the boss's role is a focus on the team mission and how it relates to company goals and results.

But, ultimately, people need to find a higher purpose for their labor. *What's our vision?* Here is the simple human need to align with an inspiring vision that adds relevance to their lives by signifying their membership in something larger than themselves.

And this is not in some framed vision statement written by committee and hung on every conference room wall, but in an ongoing discussion of what the company stands for and why, delivered with leadership conviction at every appropriate moment. After all, that *is* the work of a visionary.

Also implicit in this vision question is: how company strategy and purpose align with marketplace opportunities and challenges. That requires turning all eyes *outward* to customer needs and marketplace forces. Otherwise, how can people understand the purpose and the rules of the game? And their individual roles in the enterprise.

Finally, if all of these conditions are met (which is a vital but not nearly often enough achieved outcome) people are likely to attach themselves to a given organization. In a word they become *engaged* in their work with a willingness to contribute their discretionary effort: *How can I help?*

We must never forget that engagement is an employee *choice* that is part rational (what's in it for me?) and part emotional (I like and trust these people.) One's engagement inevitably varies from day to day and even from year to year although it typically endures at some level until a person concludes that he or she has made an unwise choice and that their commitment is misplaced.

Which raises another point. All of the above conditions are dynamic and volatile to some extent. Few people go through these transitional stages and remain forever engaged and committed, given the dynamics of today's global economy. In short, the jury is always out to some degree. Leaderships change. Market conditions fluctuate.

People move from one set of responsibilities to another. Teams add or lose personalities.

Lest you think I'm talking about some unreachable Utopia, consider that what I've outlined here is nothing more than the blocking and tackling of good leadership. It is what we have paid lip service to as leadership best practice for many years.

Questions for Today's Boss

If you want to encapsulate the employee's needs at work, they can be reduced to the following six questions that comprise what I term the Communication Leadership Model.

Responding faithfully to these questions is the essence of what it means to be a good boss:

- What's my job?
- How am I doing?
- Does anyone care?
- How are WE doing?

- What's our vision?
- How can I help?

The final remedy for what we've been examining in this discussion is a four-part strategy that includes an integrated initiative much like Pfizer's OWNIT! or the QVC Culture of Leadership.

The Essentials
What are the necessary steps in such an initiative?

First, alert the entire organization to a culture change that is people-centric.

Second, mount a training and development initiative to ensure that everyone understands and performs their assigned role.

Third, inculcate the information and insights essential to leadership within the organization's culture and communication strategy.

And fourth, deploy an integrated accountability process that makes it absolutely clear that none of this is optional and that there will be a system of rewards and penalties based on full transparency and inspection of all leadership behavior.

Accompanying all of that must be an overall educational initiative to help people understand the organization's vision, mission, and marketplace strategy.

If this strategy strikes you as a bit daunting, it is! It will require exquisite collaboration at the highest levels of an organization with a senior leadership that is fully committed. And it needs to be implemented and sustained by a staff that can reason and strategize together without regard to silo boundaries.

What's at stake is the critical need to match human development to the unfolding and unstoppable demands of technocracy. Otherwise, the technocracy will outperform and neutralize the human leadership at great cost to our collective humanity.

To get you started on the road to being the kind of boss we've postulated here, there is a multi-use questionnaire, which I refer to as eye-opening, in the appendix. I call it eye-opening because it is designed to help you recognize your strengths and weaknesses as a boss. Most of us suffer blind spots about our own behavior. The questionnaire will help you overcome those blind spots if you are scrupulously honest in your answers. I invite you to take this first step in becoming a truly good boss.

The Communication Leadership Model

Note that the questionnaire is based on the six questions of the Communication Leadership Model. Here is a graphic representation of that model. Note also that it is rendered in the form of a circle to make the point that this is a never-ending journey for both boss and employee.

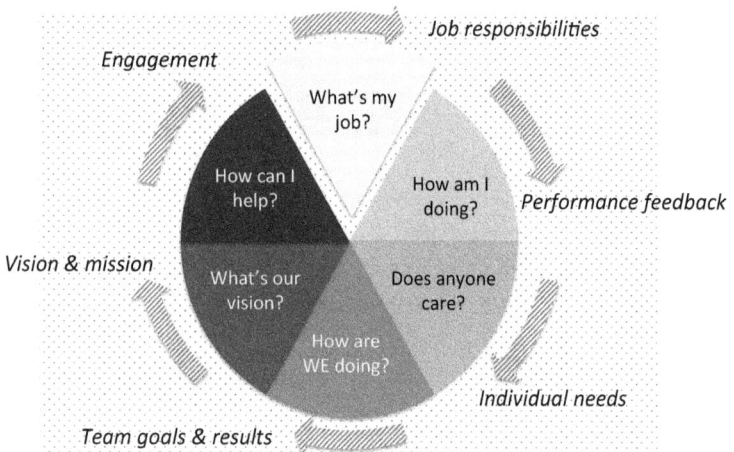

In Conclusion

I can think of no better way to close this book on bosses and their influence than to share a quote from one of my favorite leadership teachers and observers. Here's what author Gary Hamel concludes in his excellent book *The Future of Management*.

> "For the first time since the dawning of the industrial age, the only way to build a company that's fit for the future is to build one that's fit for human beings as well.
>
> "This is your opportunity to build a 21st century management model that truly elicits, honors and cherishes human initiative, creativity and passion…
>
> "Do that, and you will have built an organization that is fully human and fully prepared for the extraordinary opportunities that lie ahead."

The Rate Your Boss Questionnaire

This questionnaire has been developed to assess the effectiveness of bosses in relation to the 'Questions for Today's Boss' posed on page 96. Together, these questions constitute the Communication Leadership Model.

The questionnaire provides a straightforward way for an individual to assess their boss. It can also be used by someone interested in doing a self-assessment, who simply needs to consider what their typical team member might respond to the 30 items.

And if you are the leader of a team and wish to gather feedback on your behavior as the boss, you can share the questionnaire with team members for each of their responses. Your ability to listen objectively and to remain non-defensive may be tested, but this can be a very useful and instructive exercise, and the basis of a robust team discussion.

As an individual, here is an opportunity to rate your behaviors in relation to the six employee questions we've been considering. Your job is to answer each item as honestly as you can manage. At the end of the survey are instructions that will permit a bottom line rating on each of the six questions in the Communication Leadership Model. Also offered are ideas about actions that can be taken in response to ratings derived from this process.

Remember: the outcome of the survey will only be as accurate as your honesty in rating your behavior.

You can download a copy of the questionnaire (in the form of an Excel spreadsheet) from www.changestart.com/bosses. The spreadsheet will show the aggregated result of your responses. And the questionnaire can of course also be set up for online access through Survey Monkey or other websites providing low- or no-cost research tools.

Rate Your Boss (or Yourself)

Circle the response that most closely reflects your boss's behavior (or your own if this is a self-assessment.)

	Does the boss . . . [1=Always 2=Usually 3=Occasionally 4=Seldom 5=Never]					
1	Keep you informed about changes in job priorities	1	2	3	4	5
2	Recognize you when you've done an especially good job	1	2	3	4	5j
3	Recognize cooperation and team-work	1	2	3	4	5
4	Describe how your team's mission fits into the organization as a whole	1	2	3	4	5
5	Support your efforts even when there are risks involved	1	2	3	4	5
6	Establish a climate of openness and trust	1	2	3	4	5
7	Regularly provide feedback on how you are doing against expectations	1	2	3	4	5
8	Solicit ideas and suggestions from you and other team members	1	2	3	4	5
9	Encourage cooperation with other teams, work groups or operations	1	2	3	4	5
10	Encourage you to express your views frankly	1	2	3	4	5
11	Tell you which aspects of an assignment you handled well	1	2	3	4	5
12	Relate business strategy to the team's and your job	1	2	3	4	5
13	Explain how the team benefits customers (internal or external)	1	2	3	4	5
14	Keep feedback focused on performance, not on you as a person	1	2	3	4	5
15	Define your team's common goals and objectives	1	2	3	4	5

16	Involve you in team planning and performance discussions	1	2	3	4	5
17	Involve you in planning job changes that affect your work	1	2	3	4	5
18	Provide clear direction on what is expected of you	1	2	3	4	5
19	Explain how organizational changes and events may affect the team	1	2	3	4	5
20	Make you feel that you are part of a worthwhile organization	1	2	3	4	5
21	Listen to ideas and concerns from you and the team	1	2	3	4	5
22	Indicate which job priorities have the most importance	1	2	3	4	5
23	Discuss with you actions to improve your performance	1	2	3	4	5
24	Encourage efforts to collaborate with other teams and work groups	1	2	3	4	5
25	Help you feel your job is important to the organization	1	2	3	4	5
26	Encourage a sense of team success and cooperation	1	2	3	4	5
27	Help to remove obstacles to your efficiency and productivity	1	2	3	4	5
28	Show a willingness to listen to work group needs and find solutions	1	2	3	4	5
29	Encourage creativity and innovation on the job	1	2	3	4	5
30	Demonstrate commitment to the organization's vision and mission	1	2	3	4	5

Tabulation Key

Each of these 30 items maps to one of the six questions in the Communication Leadership Model (see page 98). Collectively, the responses yield a rating that provides an effective indicator of the extent to which the person being assessed acts in a way that ensures team members have answers to those questions.

There are five matching items for each of the questions:

- What's my job? (1, 12, 17, 18, 22)
- How am I doing? (2, 7, 11, 14, 23)
- Does anyone care? (6, 10, 20, 21, 25)
- How are WE doing? (3, 9, 15, 26, 28)
- What's our vision? (4, 13, 19, 24, 30)
- How can I help? (5, 8, 27, 29, 16)

Identify the items above that comprise each of the six questions and find the average of each group of items that match the appropriate question. For example, the total score for the five items related to "What's my job?" might be 20. The average number for that question (five items) then would be 4.

You can compare your relative strengths and potential areas for improvement on each of the six questions. You can also look at the individual items in the questionnaire as a self-reporting tool for each behavior and determine any performance gaps.

If you choose to give your team members the opportunity to fill out the companion questionnaire, you can then make comparisons between your self-evaluation and their perceptions of your communication behavior.

This is an excellent way to check your perceptions against theirs. If you and the team can handle such a dialogue comfortably and openly, this can be an excellent conversation as to how to improve team communication.

You can also draw comparisons between your results and the standard provided by Gallup and others. For example, the Gallup criteria mentioned in the text identify these qualities of good bosses:

- They motivate every single employee to engage providing a compelling vision and team mission.
- They have the assertiveness to drive outcomes and the ability to overcome adversity and resistance.
- They create a culture of clear accountability in which each team member takes responsibility for their results.

- They build relationships that create trust, open dialogue, and full transparency.
- They make decisions based on productivity, not politics.

Consider undertaking a kind of examination of conscience to ask yourself honestly how you believe you measure up to these defined criteria.

As a basis for comparing scores on each of the six questions in the Communication Leadership Model, here's a common-sense qualitative scale:

1=Very good | 2=Good | 3=Bad | 4=Very bad | 5=Ugly

A more detailed and perhaps more useful exercise might be to check your self-rating on *each* of the 30 questionnaire items using the above scale to identify *specific* leadership behaviors you need to work on.

Team Feedback
If you are gathering team feedback from a number of team members to determine how your team perceives your behavior, use the Rate Your Boss questionnaire. Give each team member a copy; ask for their candid perceptions.

The key difference is that you assign a team member to tabulate the results and summarize the findings from the team as a whole. That approach will ensure anonymity for each team member and encourage honest responses.

Be sure to average the total team input for each questionnaire item. To do so, total the results from each team member and divide by the total number of team members. Here's an example:

Step 1: Each team member tabulates their responses using the directions listed under the Tabulation Key on page 103.

Step 2: An assigned team member averages the scores to produce a result for each of the six questions in the Communication Leadership Model.

Step 3: The averaged scores are recorded for the total team.

Taking Action

Gathering and reviewing feedback on behavior under these important six categories is a crucial first step in improving the effectiveness of boss behavior.

As you consider the results from your self-analysis or from your team's feedback, first review strengths and weaknesses portrayed in the ratings under the six categories. The elements that contribute to a weak rating in one or more areas will point to changes that you could make in your approach to being the boss.

- What's my job? (1, 12, 17, 18, 22)
- How am I doing? (2, 7, 11, 14, 23)
- Does anyone care? (6, 10, 20, 21, 25)
- How are WE doing? (3, 9, 15, 26, 28)
- What's our vision? (4, 13, 19, 24, 30)
- How can I help? (5, 8, 27, 29, 16)

For example, if the rating under "How am I doing" is bad (or worse) you need to consider the five areas where there is clearly a shortfall in your actions: items 2, 7, 11, 14 and 23.

The table on the next page presents each of the questionnaire elements in the form of an action or behavior that will address weaknesses identified in the evaluation. For example, the relevant elements if the boss receives a low rating on addressing the question, "How am I doing" are therefore:

- Recognize those who do an especially good job.
- Regularly provide feedback on how team members are performing.
- Tell them which aspects of an assignment were handled well.
- Keep feedback focused on performance, not on personal attributes.
- Discuss actions to improve individual and team performance.

You will of course develop your own plans and processes (in areas such as training, coaching, communication and goal-setting) to address issues identified in the questionnaire data.

In summary, to become a good or very good boss . . .

1   Keep team members informed about changes in job priorities

2   Recognize those who do an especially good job

3   Recognize cooperation and teamwork

4   Describe how your team's mission fits into the organization as a whole

5   Support team members' efforts even when there are risks involved

6   Establish a climate of openness and trust

7   Regularly provide feedback on how team members are performing

8   Solicit ideas and suggestions

9   Encourage cooperation with other teams, work groups or operations

10   Encourage team members to express your views frankly

11   Tell team members which aspects of an assignment were handled well

12   Relate business strategy to the team's goals and individual jobs

13   Explain how the team benefits customers (internal or external)

14   Keep feedback focused on performance, not on personal attributes

15   Define your team's common goals and objectives

16   Involve team members in planning and performance discussions

17   Involve team members in planning job changes that affect their work

18   Provide clear direction on what is expected

19   Explain how organizational changes and events may affect the team

20   Make team members feel that they're part of a worthwhile organization

21   Listen to ideas and concerns from the team

22   Indicate which job priorities have the most importance

23   Discuss actions to improve individual and team performance

24   Encourage efforts to collaborate with other teams and work groups

25   Help team members feel their jobs are important to the organization

26   Encourage a sense of team success and cooperation

27   Help to remove obstacles to efficiency and productivity

28   Show a willingness to listen to work group needs, and to find solutions

29   Encourage creativity and innovation on the job

30   Demonstrate commitment to the organization's vision and mission

Making it Happen

It's evident that these actions or commitments are responses to basic human needs; and it seems almost elementary good sense that a boss should provide an environment in which these behaviors are the norm.

As we have seen from the research by Gallup and ROI reported earlier, more bosses earn negative ratings than positive. Yet the cure or solution should be neither complex nor difficult. Changing the workplace culture and dramatically improving organizational performance can be achieved by assessing boss performance against these criteria, and then training and guiding bosses to behave in a way that's aligned with the model.

ACKNOWLEDGMENTS

Every book is a collaborative effort among the author, an editorial team, and a publisher. This one is especially collaborative, with some 16 panelists contributing their boss experiences and insights. I am deeply indebted to this group for helping to shine a light on this important subject and to offer invaluable advice.

The distinguished global contributors are Angela Sinickas, Bish Mukherjee, Dan Koger, Dave Johnston, David Norris, Jim Shaffer, Kellie Garrett, Pixie Emslie, Priya Bates, Robert Libbey, Shel Holtz, Stacy Wilson, and four others who choose to remain anonymous.

Having acknowledged their giving substance from the "real" corporate world, I must emphasize that the opinions offered here are mine alone together with any flaws or other lapses.

Finally, I offer my unending gratitude to my publisher Richard Bevan. I could not have carried on this journey without his guidance at every step. He and I were once colleagues at Towers Perrin, where he was one of the truly great bosses in an admirable corporate culture.

I have been privileged to witness and participate in one of the most remarkable periods of change in the history of American business. It was one hell of a ride!

www.ingramcontent.com/pod-product-compliance
Lightning Source LLC
Chambersburg PA
CBHW060620200326
41521CB00007B/833